a new spin on
# CURVED
piecing

# The technique is easy. The results are fabulous!

If you've ever machine pieced curved seams, you know how tedious the piecing can be. Not any longer! Joyce Cambron's **New Spin On Curved Piecing** technique brings enjoyment to curved piecing. Her unique method simplifies the process while producing remarkably accurate results.

Joyce begins by pressing freezer paper templates onto the right side of her fabric. Then, leaving wide seam allowances, she cuts out the shapes which she calls "wedges."

Next, she presses under the concave seam allowances of the wedges. Matching the pressed concave edge of one wedge to the flat convex edge of its neighbor, she applies a dab of basting glue to hold the pieces in place while she stitches in the pressed creases. The result is a precisely pieced seam!

Now you can make unusual and beautiful quilted projects and have lots of fun in the process. Beginning on page 4, follow **Getting Started**, which includes a step-by-step **Practice Lesson**. You'll even make a pair of Scallop Placemats as you go!

## EDITORIAL STAFF

**EDITOR-IN-CHIEF:** Susan White Sullivan
**CRAFT PUBLICATIONS DIRECTOR:** Cheryl Johnson
**SPECIAL PROJECTS DIRECTOR:** Susan Frantz Wiles
**SENIOR PREPRESS DIRECTOR:** Mark Hawkins
**ART PUBLICATIONS DIRECTOR:** Rhonda Shelby
**TECHNICAL WRITER:** Jean Lewis
**TECHNICAL ASSOCIATES:** Frances Huddleston, Mary Hutcheson, and Lisa Lancaster
**EDITORIAL WRITER:** Susan McManus Johnson
**ART CATEGORY MANAGER:** Lora Puls
**GRAPHIC DESIGNER:** Jacob Casleton
**GRAPHIC ARTIST:** Janie Marie Wright
**IMAGING TECHNICIAN:** Stephanie Johnson
**PHOTOGRAPHY MANAGER:** Katherine Laughlin
**CONTRIBUTING PHOTOSTYLIST:** Sondra Daniel
**CONTRIBUTING PHOTOGRAPHERS:** Mark Mathews and Ken West
**PUBLISHING SYSTEMS ADMINISTRATOR:** Becky Riddle
**MAC INFORMATION TECHNOLOGY SPECIALIST:** Robert Young

## BUSINESS STAFF

**PRESIDENT AND CHIEF EXECUTIVE OFFICER:** Rick Barton
**VICE PRESIDENT AND CHIEF OPERATIONS OFFICER:** Tom Siebenmorgen
**VICE PRESIDENT OF SALES:** Mike Behar
**DIRECTOR OF FINANCE AND ADMINISTRATION:** Laticia Mull Dittrich
**NATIONAL SALES DIRECTOR:** Martha Adams
**INFORMATION TECHNOLOGY DIRECTOR:** Hermine Linz
**CONTROLLER:** Francis Caple
**VICE PRESIDENT, OPERATIONS:** Jim Dittrich
**RETAIL CUSTOMER SERVICE MANAGER:** Stan Raynor
**PRINT PRODUCTION MANAGER:** Fred F. Pruss

Library of Congress Control Number: 2010930476
ISBN-13: 978-1-60900-071-4

# Setting the Curve for Success

Joyce Cambron and her husband live at the edge of the Sawtooth Wilderness Area in Idaho, less than three hours from Boise.

"Our cabin is at 5000 feet," says Joyce. "Outside my window is a wall of mountain, the peak of which is 9000 feet high. We have elk, deer, wolves—all kinds of wildlife have been spotted around here. We see a lot of hummingbirds at our feeders."

When she isn't developing new quilt patterns in this inspirational setting, Joyce sells her patterns at the quilt shop where she works.

"It's fun to work and teach at the shop," she says. "It helps me keep a pulse on what's happening in the world of quilting.

"I've dabbled in lots of creative media, but quilting has been my main interest since before my youngest son was born nineteen years ago."

Joyce's fun new approach to curved piecing is the culmination of two of her own learning experiences. "I took a seminar taught by Judy Mathieson on paper-piecing Mariner's Compass quilts. I combined what I learned with a hand appliqué technique to make this new way of piecing curves really easy. When I taught this method, each student came to the second class with a completed block. This method really satisfied his or her expectations. There's simply no reason to be afraid of piecing curves anymore."

Joyce has a new Web site under construction so visitors can view her latest quilts, patterns, and other creations at SeamsLikeFunQuilts.com.

3

Are you ready to learn an amazing technique that will have you piecing accurate curves and creating exciting new projects? Take a minute to read through *Getting Started* and then you will be ready to begin the Practice Lesson on page 8.

## TOOLS AND SUPPLIES

*You will need the usual quilting tools and supplies, such as fabric scissors, a cutting mat, rotary cutter, and clear acrylic rulers. The supply list for each project may contain other supplies specific to that project.*

*In addition, you will need these tools and supplies:*

- Freezer paper*
- Black fine-point Sharpie® or Pilot® permanent marker
- Fine-point water-soluble fabric marker or wash-out fabric pencil
- Scissors for cutting paper
- Spray bottle of water or a container of water and a small craft paintbrush
- Rotating ironing surface (optional)
- Roxanne™ Glue-Baste-It
- Presser feet: open-toe, $1/4$", and walking foot

* Rolls of freezer paper can usually be found in grocery stores with aluminum foil and plastic wrap. Quilt shops often carry $8^1/2$" x 11" sheets of freezer paper, but because the rolls are 18" wide, they are better suited for working with the patterns in this book.

# READING THE PATTERNS

*Patterns are printed with numbers/letters and markings to help with cutting, placement, and piecing. Not every pattern will have all of the markings. Patterns are printed right side up and do not include seam allowances.*

***Pattern pieces*** forming the main designs are referred to as **wedges**. When a wedge is composed of several smaller pieces, those pieces are called **sub-wedges**.

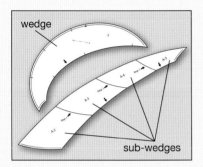

***Numbers/Letters*** indicate pattern name. Numbers also indicate position as shown on Figs. and Diagrams.

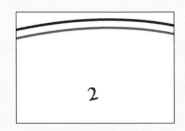

***Black Solid Lines*** are tracing/cutting lines.

***Grey Arrows*** indicate template placement. Place arrow on straight grain of fabric.

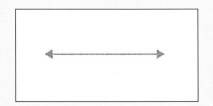

***Dark Pink Lines*** indicate edges where placement lines will be drawn around the templates on the seam allowances during construction.

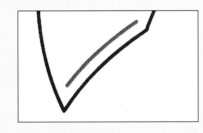

***Red Short Lines*** are registration marks used to align wedges when piecing.

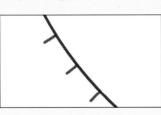

***Black Arrows*** point to the edge where a seam allowance will be turned under during construction. If a template has more than one edge to turn under or if an edge will be turned after joining multiple wedges, the arrows may also have a Step Number to indicate the order in which they will be turned under.

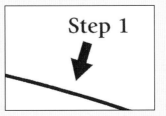

***Grey Dashed Lines and Colored Arrows*** indicate a pattern with multiple pieces to be joined to make a whole pattern.

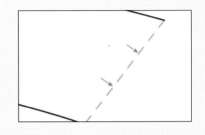

***Red Triangles*** indicate where to stop gluing and stitching when piecing. They are also used to indicate pivot points when sewing. If there are no triangles along a seam allowance, the seam will be stitched from edge to edge.

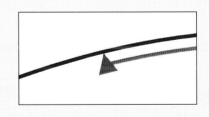

***Black Dashed Lines*** indicate that a template will be cut from a strip set. The dashed line will be placed on the seam of the strip set.

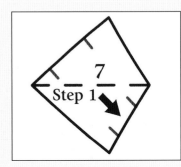

## WORKING WITH FREEZER PAPER

- Freezer paper has a dull (paper) side and a shiny (wax) side. Always trace, mark, or write on the **dull** side of the paper using a black fine-point *permanent* marker.

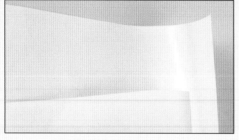

**TIP**

Some markers, especially colors, may bleed when pressed with a hot iron. To test a marker, write on a small piece of freezer paper; then press the paper onto a fabric scrap. Remove the paper and check the fabric for ink smears or bleeding.

- When pressing freezer paper templates onto fabric, always place the **shiny** side on the **right** side of the fabric and press on the dull side.

- To trace large patterns, it may be necessary to join two or more pieces of freezer paper. To join, place pieces, dull side up, on an ironing surface and overlap the edges 1". Using the tip of an iron, press along the overlapped edges only. Carefully lift paper (seam may adhere to ironing surface) and treat the joined papers as a single sheet.

- To repair a torn template, simply cut a "band aid" from freezer paper and press it in place over the tear. Transfer any labels or markings onto the repair.

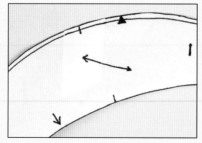

- Unless joining or repairing pieces of freezer paper, never press the shiny side to itself or to any other paper. Freezer paper easily peels away from most fabrics but may adhere permanently to paper.

## MAKING AND USING TEMPLATES

- To trace a pattern, place a piece of freezer paper over the pattern and trace over the solid black lines. Trace each pattern as many times as indicated in project instructions for each fabric.

**TIP**

Use removable tape to secure freezer paper to pattern page to keep paper from shifting while tracing.

- Once traced onto freezer paper, patterns are referred to as templates.

- If the instructions call for a template to be cut in reverse, it is because it will be used in the opposite direction. Trace the pattern onto plain white paper; flip the pattern over and trace onto freezer paper as many times as indicated in project instructions for each fabric.

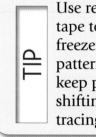

- Transfer *all* pattern numbers and markings to traced patterns.

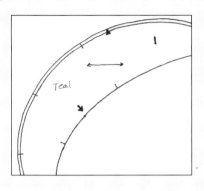

> **TIP**
>
> Keeping the cut fabric pieces clearly labeled and organized makes construction quicker and easier. So, in addition to the pattern markings, label each traced pattern with a short description of the fabric you plan to use for that piece. For example, red print, purple stripe, or teal solid.

- Use paper scissors to cut out templates exactly on drawn lines.

- Always allow at least 1" between shapes when positioning templates on fabric.

- Unless otherwise indicated by a grey arrow on the pattern, position templates on fabric with the longest *concave* curve on the bias.

- To cut fabric pieces using templates, press the templates onto the **right** side of the fabric, using a hot, dry iron. **Do not** remove templates until instructed.
- When cutting out fabric wedges, unless otherwise noted in project instructions, add wide ($3/8$"- $1/2$") seam allowances for all **curved** edges of wedges, narrow ($1/4$") seam allowances for **center ovals** or **circles**, and accurate $1/4$" seam allowances for all **straight** edges.

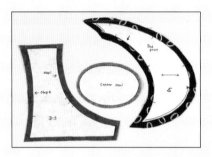

> **TIP**
>
> Wider seam allowances on the wedges are easier to handle when turning, pressing, and gluing. Seam allowances can be trimmed to $1/4$" after wedges or sub-wedges are sewn together.

*Now that you know the basics, let's get started making a set of placemats!*

# PRACTICE LESSON: SCALLOP PLACEMATS

This lesson allows you to learn the **New Spin On Curved Piecing** technique. You may simply study the steps before beginning one of the other projects in the book, but completing the placemats will give you a better understanding of the technique and a chance to practice the skills needed.

## FABRIC REQUIREMENTS

*Yardage is based on 43"/44" (109 cm/112 cm) wide fabric. Yardage and instructions are for 2 placemats made from 4 fabrics.*

    ³/₈ yd (34 cm) **each** of 4 different print fabrics

    ⁵/₈ yd (57 cm) of fabric for backing

*You will also need:*

    Roxanne™ Glue-Baste-It

    Fabric glue stick

    Two 22" x 16½" (56 cm x 42 cm) rectangles of lightweight cotton batting, Pellon® Fusible Fleece, or Insul-Bright™, a product that will make the placemats heat-resistant.

## CUTTING THE PIECES

*Refer to **Making And Using Templates**, page 6, to use patterns, pages 13-15, to make templates. When cutting, add ³/₈" – ¹/₂" seam allowances to **wedges** and a ¹/₄" seam allowance to **center oval**. Refer to **Rotary Cutting**, page 72, for all other cutting.*

**From print fabric #1:**
- Cut 2 **wedges** from *each* template 1, 3, and 5.

**From print fabric #2:**
- Cut 2 **wedges** from *each* template 2, 4, and 6.

**From print fabric #3:**
- Cut 2 **wedges** from *each* template 1, 3, and 5.

**From print fabric #4:**
- Cut 2 **wedges** from *each* template 2, 4, and 6.

**From 1 print fabric:**
- Cut 2 **center ovals**.

**From backing fabric:**
- Cut 4 **backing rectangles** 11¹/₄" x 16¹/₂".

## PRESSING SEAM ALLOWANCES

1. Using the edge of the template as a guide, finger press the *concave* edge (indicated by the thick black arrow) of 1 **wedge 1** to the wrong side (**Fig. 1**).

**Fig. 1**

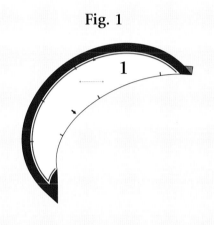

2. If there are sections of the seam allowance that will not turn under easily, make shallow clips in the seam allowance about every ¹/₂" to 1" (**Fig. 2**).

**Fig. 2**

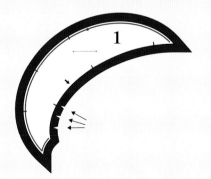

3. Use the tip of an iron to firmly press the finger-pressed seam allowance to the wrong side (**Fig. 3**).

**Fig. 3**

> **TIP**
> For an even sharper crease, spray the seam allowance with water or use a paintbrush to apply water to the seam allowance when pressing.

4. Repeat Steps 1-3 to press under the *concave* seam allowances of remaining wedges (total of 24 wedges).

## GLUING

1. Referring to **Placement Diagram**, arrange wedges into an oval.

**Placement Diagram**

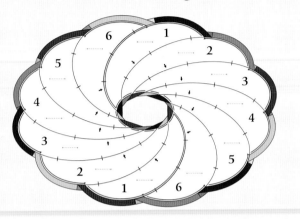

2. Select 1 wedge 1 and 1 wedge 2 from oval. Place small dots of glue on the *convex* seam allowance of wedge 2, about ¹/₄" apart and as close to the edge of the template as possible (**Fig. 4**). **Note: Do not** apply glue beyond the red triangle on the template.

**Fig. 4**

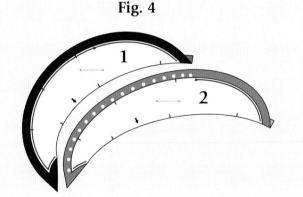

3. Matching registration marks, position the pressed edge of wedge 1 over the glue dots on wedge 2; firmly finger-press in place (**Fig. 5**). In the same manner, continue adding wedges 3-6 to make **Unit 1**. Make 4 Unit 1's.

**Fig. 5**

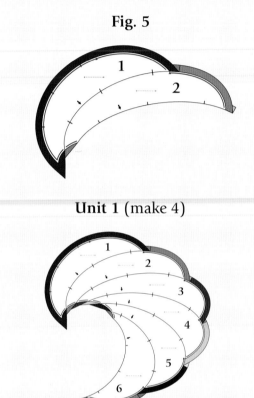

**Unit 1** (make 4)

4. Use water-soluble fabric marker or wash-out pencil to draw around templates onto the seam allowance of each Unit 1 where indicated by the dark pink lines on the templates. Place a dot on the seam allowance where indicated by each red triangle (**Fig. 6**).

**Fig. 6**

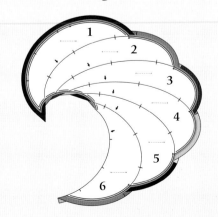

## STITCHING

*For better visibility when sewing, use an open-toe presser foot.*

1. Gently remove templates from each Unit 1.

> **TIP** If templates are difficult to remove, press briefly with a hot iron and remove while paper is still warm.

2. On 1 Unit 1, fold back wedge 1 to expose the crease between wedge 1 and 2. With wedge 1 on top, position the narrow end (the end that faces the center of the placemat) under the presser foot (**Fig. 7**). Stitch in the crease, stopping at marked dot; press. Repeat to sew seams between each wedge of Unit 1.

**Fig. 7**

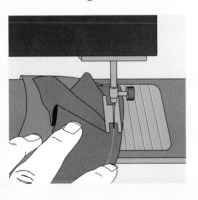

> **TIP** If your crease is hard to see, use your water-soluble fabric marker or wash-out fabric pencil to draw exactly on the crease before stitching.

3. Repeat Step 2 to sew each seam of each remaining Unit 1.

4. To join 2 Unit 1's, place dots of glue on the *convex* seam allowances of each wedge 1 (**Fig. 8**). **Note: Do not** apply glue beyond the marked dot.

**Fig. 8**

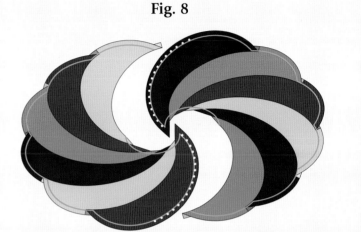

5. Position the pressed edge of wedge 6 over the glue dots on wedge 1; press firmly in place to make **Unit 2**. Make 2 Unit 2's.

**Unit 2** (make 2)

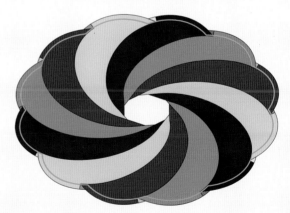

6. Repeat Step 2 to sew seams between wedges 1 and 6 of each Unit 2.

7. Trim stitched seam allowances to $1/4$". **Note:** While seam allowances do not have to be trimmed, doing so will reduce bulk and make quilting easier. If trimming seam allowances, always trim after a seam has been sewn but before it is crossed by another seam.

## ATTACHING THE CENTER OVAL OR CIRCLE

*Use this technique for all projects that have center ovals or circles.*

1. With template and fabric facing down, apply **glue stick** to a small section (1"-1$^1/_2$" long) of the seam allowance. Using the edge of the template as a guide, use the tip of a seam ripper, stiletto, or wooden skewer to gently but firmly fold the seam allowance to the wrong side (**Fig. 9**). Continue gluing and folding seam allowance in small sections until entire seam allowance is folded back. Repeat for remaining center oval.

**Fig. 9**

> **TIP**
> It may take a little practice to achieve smooth edges on a circle or oval. If your first attempt is not as smooth as you would like, simply remove the template, press it onto another piece of fabric, and try again.

2. Place drops of basting glue on center opening seam allowances of 1 Unit 2, close to the drawn line. Aligning folded edges of center oval with drawn line, finger-press center oval onto Unit 2 to make **placemat top**. Make 2 placemat tops.

**Placemat Top** (make 2)

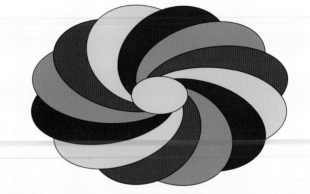

> **TIP**
> You can wait until you are quilting the placemats to topstitch around the center ovals, or if desired, you can stitch the center oval in place now using your preferred **Appliqué** method, page 73.

## LAYERING AND BASTING

1. If using cotton batting or Insul-Brite, center each placemat top, right side up, on a batting rectangle. Refer to **Assembling the Quilt**, page 75, to pin-baste layers. If using fusible fleece, center each placemat top, right side up, on fusible side of fleece rectangle. Follow manufacturer's instructions to fuse placemat top to fleece, being careful not to touch iron to any exposed adhesive.

2. Fold back and pin the small flap of fabric at each marked dot around the outside edge of the placemat top (**Fig. 10**).

**Fig. 10**

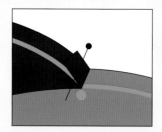

3. Using a high contrast thread color in the bobbin and pivoting at marked dots, stitch just outside drawn outer lines on placemat top.

## FINISHING

1. To sew 2 **backing rectangles** together to make **backing**, match long edges and right sides. Begin stitching with a normal stitch length for approximately 4". Backstitch and switch to a long basting stitch for approximately 5". Backstitch again and switch back to normal stitch length to complete the seam. Leave the basting stitches in place until you are ready to turn the placemat. Make 2 backings.

**Backing** (make 2)

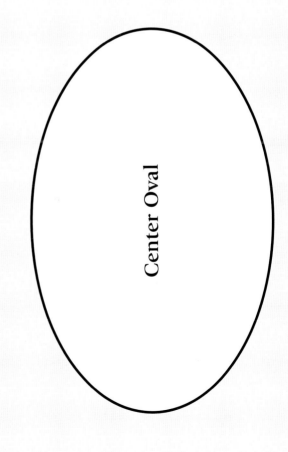

2. Matching right sides, center placemat top on backing. Stitching just inside previous stitching line and pivoting at marked dots, sew backing and placemat top together around outer edges; remove pins. Leaving a $1/4$" seam allowance, trim excess batting and backing. Clip up to, but not through, stitching at each marked dot. Repeat using remaining placemat top and backing.

3. Remove basting stitches in backing seam. Turn placemat right side out; press. Hand stitch opening closed.
4. Refer to **Quilting**, page 74, to quilt placemats as desired. The models are outline quilted around each wedge. The center oval is outline quilted just inside the folded edge.

*Now that you have finished your placemats, you are ready to move on to your next project! As you look through the instructions you will notice that the Figs. and Diagrams do not always show seam allowances and templates. Sometimes it is easier to see the construction without seam allowances and templates. You will still need to add seam allowances as you cut and leave templates attached until instructed to remove.*

Center Oval

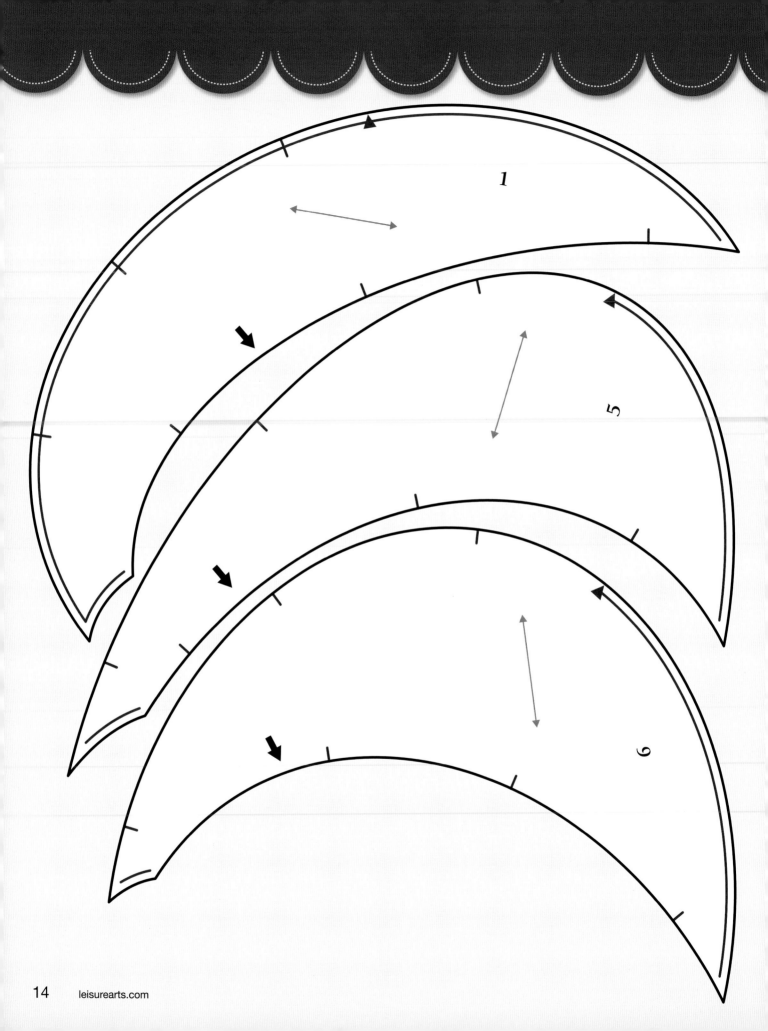

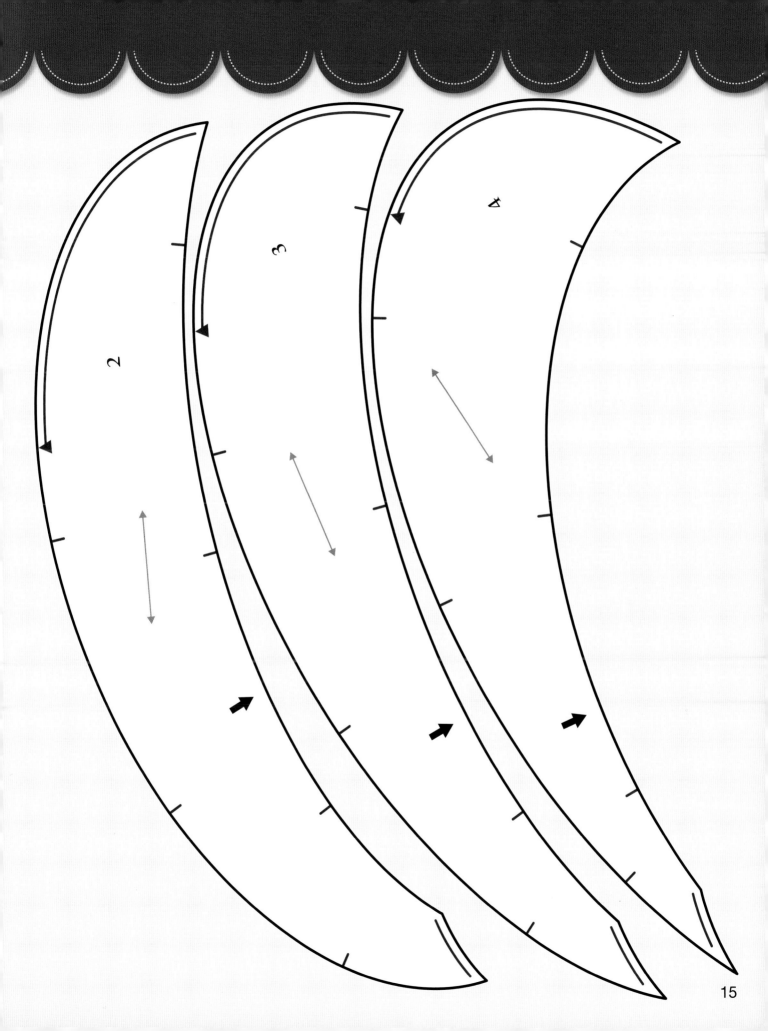

# AUTUMN LEAVES

This pillow, with its clean contemporary design, makes the perfect addition to a fall decorating scheme. The large pieces go together quickly making it a good beginner project. To change colors with the seasons, substitute pretty pastels for spring, bold brights for summer, or festive reds and greens for winter.

## FABRIC REQUIREMENTS

*Yardage is based on 43"/44" (109 cm/112 cm)
wide fabric. Fat quarters are approximately 21" x 18"
(53 cm x 46 cm).*

> 1 fat quarter **each** of light green, green, gold,
> and brown prints
> ¹/₂ yd (46 cm) of dark brown print (includes
> backing)
> ⁵/₈ yd (57 cm) of fabric for lining

*You will also need:*

> 20¹/₂" x 20¹/₂" (52 cm x 52 cm) square of batting
> 16" x 16" (41 cm x 41 cm) pillow form
> Roxanne™ Glue-Baste-It

## CUTTING THE PIECES

*Refer to **Making And Using Templates**, page 6, to use
patterns, pages 19-23. When cutting out pieces, add
³/₈" – ¹/₂" to all **curved** edges and ¹/₄" seam allowances
to all **straight** edges. Refer to **Rotary Cutting**, page 72,
for all other cutting. All pieces given as measurements
include seam allowances.*

**From light green print:**
- Cut 1 **wedge** using template A-1.
- Cut 1 **wedge** using template A-3.
- Cut 1 **wedge** using template B-1.
- Cut 1 **wedge** using template B-3.
- Cut 1 **wedge** using template C-1.
- Cut 1 **wedge** using template C-3.

**From green print:**
- Cut 1 **wedge** using template A-2.
- Cut 1 **wedge** using template B-2.
- Cut 1 **wedge** using template C-2.
- Cut 1 **wedge** using template G.

**From gold print:**
- Cut 1 **wedge** using template F.

**From brown print:**
- Cut 1 **wedge** using template D.
- Cut 1 **wedge** using template E.

**From dark brown print:**
- Cut 2 **side borders** 1¹/₂" x 16¹/₂".
- Cut 2 **top/bottom borders** 1¹/₂" x 18¹/₂".
- Cut 2 **backs** 18¹/₂" x 11¹/₂".

**From lining fabric:**
- Cut 1 **front lining** 20¹/₂" x 20¹/₂".

## MAKING THE PILLOW FRONT

*Refer to **Getting Started**, page 4, and **Practice
Lesson**, page 8, for techniques. When instructed
to glue and then sew wedges or Units, you will
need to glue seam, loosen or remove the templates
of adjoining wedges, sew the seam, and then
re-attach the templates.*

> *Note: Our Figs. and Diagrams are shown without
> templates and seam allowances. Your wedges will have
> templates attached and seam allowances showing.*

1. Press under the Step 1 edge of **wedge A-1**.
   Glue and then sew wedge A-1 and **wedge A-2**
   together to make **Unit 1**.

**Unit 1**

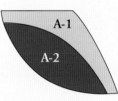

2. Press under the Step 1 edge of **wedge A-3**.
   Glue and then sew wedge A-3 and Unit 1
   together to make **Unit 2**.

**Unit 2**

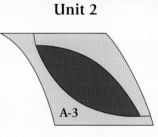

3. Repeat Steps 1 and 2 using templates **B-1**, **B-2**,
   and **B-3** to make **Unit 3**.

**Unit 3**

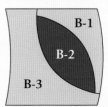

17

4. Repeat Steps 1 and 2 using templates **C-1**, **C-2**, and **C-3** to make **Unit 4**.

**Unit 4**

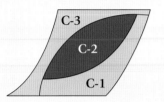

5. Using a $1/4$" seam allowance, sew Units 2, 3, and 4 together to make **Unit 5**.

**Unit 5**

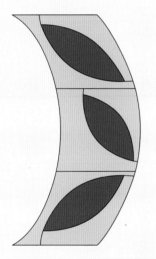

6. Press under the Step 2 edge of **Unit 5**. Glue and then sew Unit 5 to **wedge D** to make **Unit 6**.

**Unit 6**

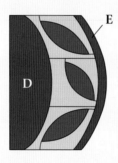

7. Press under the Step 1 edge of **wedge E**. Glue and then sew wedge E to **Unit 6** to make **Unit 7**.

**Unit 7**

8. Press under the Step 1 edge of **wedge F**. Glue and then sew wedge F to **Unit 7** to make **Unit 8**.

**Unit 8**

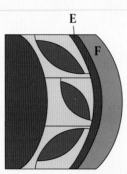

9. Press under the Step 1 edge of **wedge G**. Glue and then sew wedge G to **Unit 8** to make **Pillow Front Center**. Remove templates.

**Pillow Front Center**

10. Sew **side**, then **top/bottom borders** to pillow front center to make **Pillow Front**.

**Pillow Front**

## ASSEMBLING THE PILLOW

*Match right sides and use a $1/4$" seam allowance unless otherwise noted.*

1. Refer to **Quilting**, page 74, to mark, layer, and quilt Pillow Front, **batting**, and **front lining** as desired. The model is quilted in the ditch between each wedge. There is a leaf and vine pattern quilted in the light green background fabric around the leaves. There are quilting lines spaced $1$" – $2^1/4$" apart that follow the curve in each remaining large wedge.
2. Trim batting and lining even with pillow top.
3. Press 1 long edge of each pillow back $1/4$" to the wrong side twice. Topstitch hem close to the folded edges.
4. With right sides facing up, overlap the two hemmed edges of the pillow backs until the overall measurement is $18^1/2$" x $18^1/2$". Baste the overlapped edges together.
5. Using a $1/2$" seam allowance, sew pillow front and back together to make **Pillow**. Clip corners and turn right side out. Topstitch around pillow on inside edge of border. Insert pillow form.

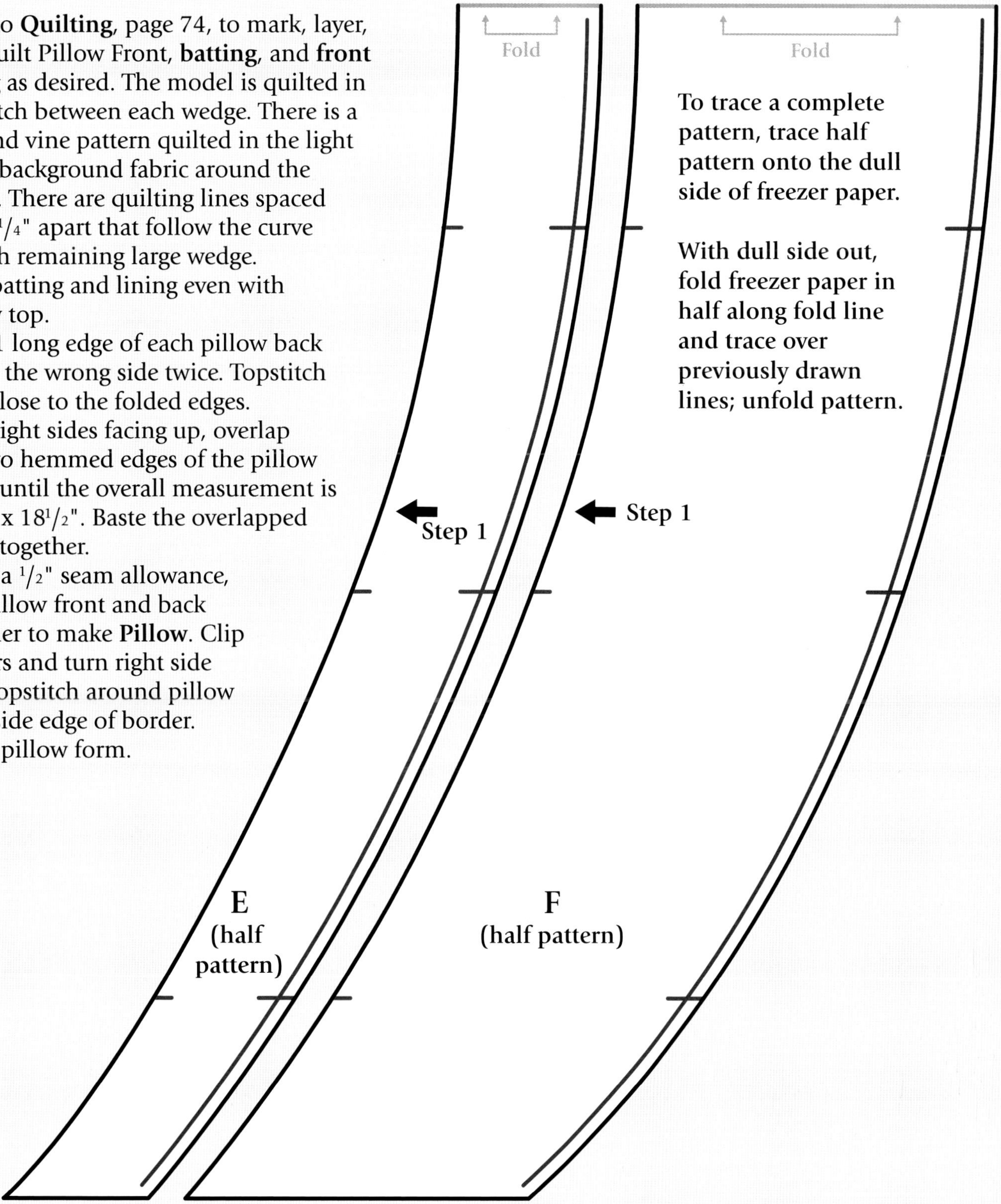

Fold

Fold

To trace a complete pattern, trace half pattern onto the dull side of freezer paper.

With dull side out, fold freezer paper in half along fold line and trace over previously drawn lines; unfold pattern.

← Step 1

← Step 1

E
(half pattern)

F
(half pattern)

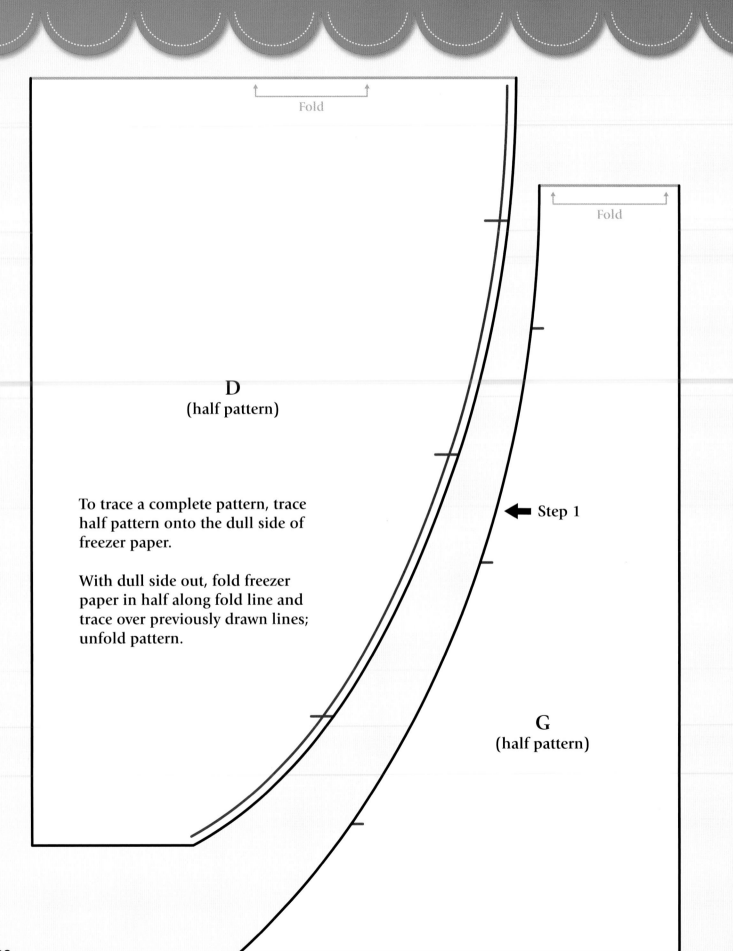

**D**
(half pattern)

**Fold**

**Fold**

To trace a complete pattern, trace half pattern onto the dull side of freezer paper.

With dull side out, fold freezer paper in half along fold line and trace over previously drawn lines; unfold pattern.

← Step 1

**G**
(half pattern)

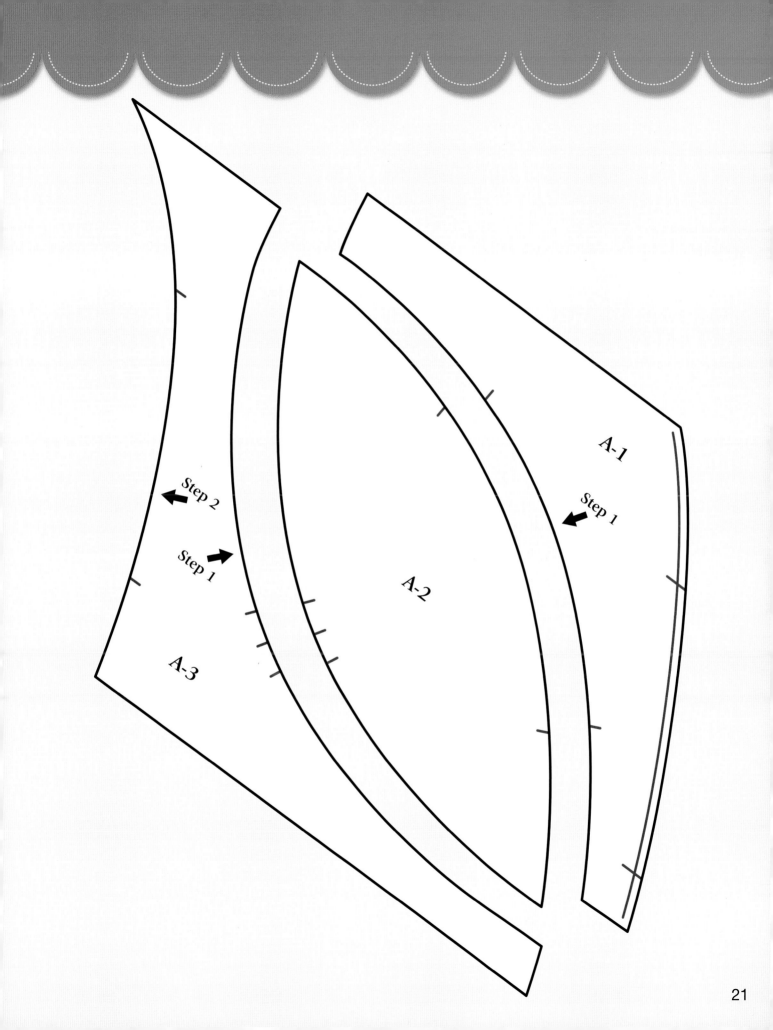

A-1

A-2

A-3

Step 1

Step 2

Step 1

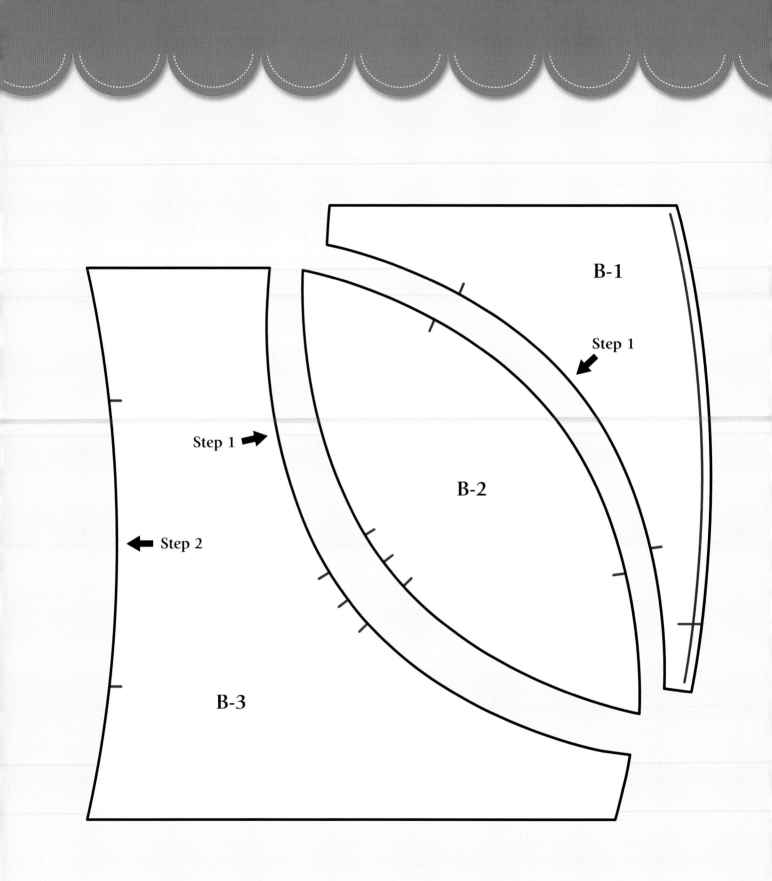

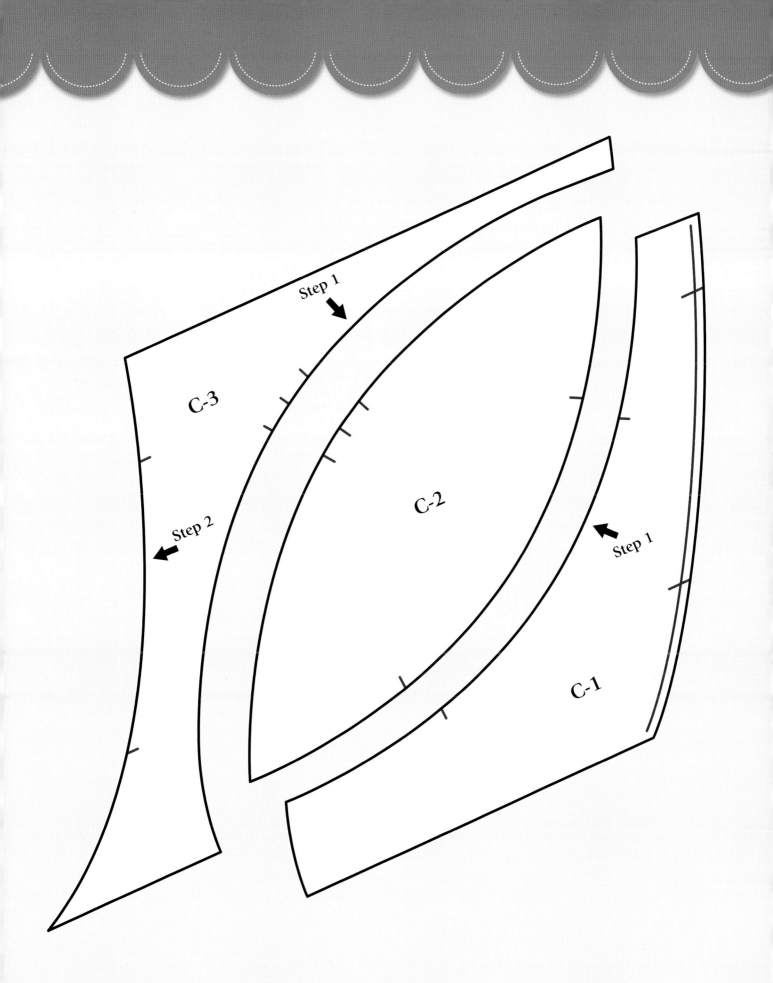

# KAYZIE DAISY

Whether you are off to a quilting class, a trip to the farmer's market, or just running errands, the roomy Kayzie Daisy tote can handle all your important belongings and purchases. An easy-to-access large outer pocket and three inner pockets make it a snap to keep up with small items like your keys, cell phone, or wallet. The fun daisy design looks great in any color combination.

## FABRIC REQUIREMENTS

*Yardage is based on 43"/44" (109 cm/112 cm) wide fabric.*

$1/4$ yd (23 cm) **each** of at least 4 assorted pink print fabrics for petals

$7/8$ yd (80 cm) of large floral print for bag front and sides, back pocket, and straps

1 yd (91 cm) of pink stripe for bag back, strap linings, outside pocket lining, and inside pockets

4" x 11" (10 cm x 28 cm) rectangle of pink/brown dot print for back pocket cuff

$5/8$ yd (57 cm) of brown print for piping, inner borders, and daisy center

$1^3/8$ yds (1.3 m) of light pink dot print for lining and daisy background

$1^1/2$ yds (1.4 m) of muslin

*You will also need:*

Compass capable of drawing a 12" (30 cm) diameter circle *or* a pencil, thumbtack, and string

$1^1/8$ yds (1 m) of 45" (114 cm) wide fusible batting

5 yds (4.6 m) of $1/16$" (2 mm) diameter piping cord

4" (10 cm) of $1/4$"w (6 mm) elastic

Roxanne™ Glue-Baste-It

## CUTTING THE PIECES

*Refer to **Making And Using Templates**, page 6, to use patterns, page 31, to make templates. When cutting out pieces, add a $1/4$" seam allowance to **center circle**. Refer to **Rotary Cutting**, page 72, for all other cutting. All pieces given as measurements include seam allowances.*

**From assorted pink print fabrics:**
- Cut 16 assorted **bias strips** $2^1/2$" x 7".

**From large floral print:**
- Cut 1 **back pocket** 11" x 11".
- Cut 2 **straps** $2^1/2$" x 28".
- Cut 2 **top outer borders** 2" x $20^1/2$".
- Cut 1 **bottom outer border** 4" x $20^1/2$".
- Cut 1 **bag bottom** 4" x $20^1/2$".
- Cut 2 **bag sides** 4" x $19^1/2$".
- Cut 2 **side outer borders** $3^1/2$" x $14^1/2$".

**From pink stripe:**
- Cut 2 **strap linings** $2^1/2$" x 28".
- Cut 1 **bag back** $20^1/2$" x 18".
- Cut 1 **back pocket lining** 11" x 11".
- Cut 1 **large inside pocket** $10^3/4$" x $7^1/2$".
- Cut 1 **medium inside pocket** $5^1/4$" x $6^1/2$".
- Cut 1 **small inside pocket** 5" x $6^1/2$".

**From brown print:**
- Cut 1 **piping square** 18" x 18".
- Cut 2 **top/bottom inner borders** 1" x $14^1/2$".
- Cut 2 **side inner borders** 1" x $13^1/2$".
- Cut 1 **center circle**, using pattern, page 31.

**From light pink dot print:**
- Cut 1 strip $3^1/2$" wide. From this strip, cut 8 squares $3^1/2$" x $3^1/2$". Cut each square once diagonally to make 16 **background triangles**.
- Cut 2 **front/back linings** $20^1/2$" x $19^1/2$".
- Cut 2 **side linings** 4" x $19^1/2$".
- Cut 1 **background square** 15" x 15".
- Cut 1 **bottom lining** 4" x $20^1/2$".

**From muslin:**
- Cut 2 **front/back backings** 22" x 21".
- Cut 2 **side backings** 5" x $20^1/2$".
- Cut 2 **bottom backing** 5" x $21^1/2$".

**From fusible batting:**
- Cut 2 **front/backs** 20" x 19".
- Cut 2 **straps** 2" x 28".
- Cut 2 **sides** $3^1/2$" x 19".
- Cut 1 **bottom** $3^1/2$" x 20".

**From freezer paper:**
- Cut 1 **square** 14" x 14".
- Cut 16 **wedge templates** using pattern, page 31.

## MAKING THE DAISY

*Refer to **Getting Started**, page 4, and **Practice Lesson**, page 8, for techniques. When instructed to glue and then sew wedges or Units, you will need to loosen or remove the templates of adjoining wedges, sew the seam, and then re-attach the templates.*

*Note: Our Figs. and Diagrams are shown without templates and seam allowances. Your wedges will have templates attached and seam allowances showing.*

### DAISY

1. Sew 1 **background triangle** to 1 **bias strip**. Clip the seam allowance at the end of the stitching (**Fig. 1**), removing the point of the triangle. Press the seam allowance open to make **Unit 1**. Make 16 Unit 1's.

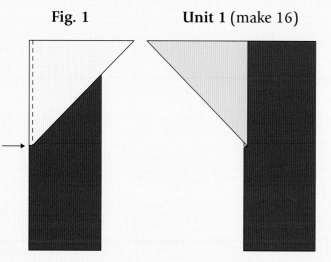

**Fig. 1**    **Unit 1** (make 16)

2. Aligning dashed line on wedge template with seamline, press 1 template to each Unit 1 (**Fig. 2**). Cut out, leaving a $3/8$" - $1/2$" seam allowance where possible. Use water-soluble fabric marker or wash-out pencil to draw around templates onto the seam allowances of each wedge where indicated by dark pink lines on templates.

**Fig. 2**

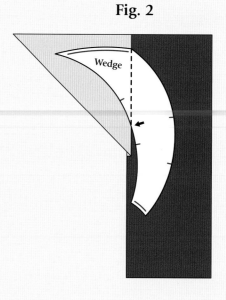

Wedge

3. Press under *concave* seam allowance of each wedge as indicated by arrow on template.

4. Mixing fabrics randomly, glue and sew 8 wedges together to make **half daisy**. Make 2 half daises.

**Half Daisy** (make 2)

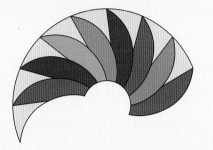

5. Remove freezer paper templates. Glue and then sew the two half daises together to make **daisy**.

**Daisy**

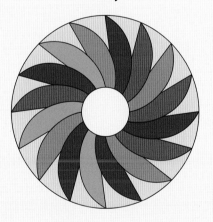

6. Refer to **Attaching The Center Oval or Circle**, page 12, to attach **center circle** to center of **daisy**. Using your preferred method, **Appliqué**, page 73, the center circle in place.

**BACKGROUND**

1. Measure across the center of the daisy from outer drawn line to outer drawn line in 3 places (**Fig. 3**). From these measurements, determine **average diameter**. Divide average diameter by 2 to determine **radius**. For example, the average diameter of **Fig. 3** is 12" and the radius is 6".

**Fig. 3**

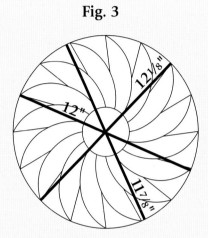

2. Fold **freezer paper square** in half horizontally and vertically and mark center; unfold.
3. Place point of compass on center mark to draw a circle using determined radius. *Note:* To make a compass, tie a length of string to a pencil. Insert a thumbtack in the string at determined radius. Place thumbtack through center mark of freezer paper square. Holding string taut, draw a circle.

> **TIP**
> The diameter of the drawn circle should measure the same as the average diameter determined in Step 1.

4. Cut out circle on drawn line; discard circle. The remaining piece is your background template. Aligning center opening of background template with drawn line of daisy, place template over daisy to check size (**Fig. 4**).

**Fig. 4**

5. If opening of template is too small and points of daisy are cut off, trim opening to the size needed. If opening is too big, repeat Steps 1-4 to re-measure daisy and cut another template.
6. Fold **background square** in half horizontally and vertically and crease; unfold.
7. Aligning crease lines, press background template onto **right side** of background square (**Fig. 5**).

**Fig. 5**

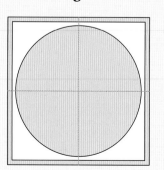

8. Using inner edge of template as a guide and leaving a $^3/_8$" to $^1/_2$" seam allowance, cut out center of background square.
9. With template side down and clipping as needed, press seam allowance to the wrong side around opening (**Fig. 6**).

**Fig. 6**

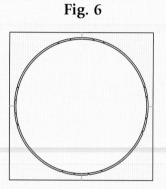

10. Referring to **Unit 2 Diagram**, align pressed edge of background square with drawn line of daisy.

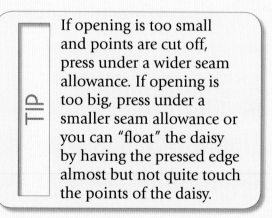

TIP

If opening is too small and points are cut off, press under a wider seam allowance. If opening is too big, press under a smaller seam allowance or you can "float" the daisy by having the pressed edge almost but not quite touch the points of the daisy.

11. When satisfied with opening size and placement, glue and then sew background square and daisy together to make **Unit 2**. Remove background template.

**Unit 2**

## ASSEMBLING THE BAG

*Match right sides and use a $^1/_4$" seam allowance unless otherwise noted. When instructed to fuse, follow fusible batting manufacturer's instructions.*

### PIPING

1. Use **piping square** and follow **Making A Continuous Bias Strip**, page 77, Steps 1-7, to make approximately 5 yds of $1^1/_4$" wide **bias strip**.
2. Lay **piping cord** in center of wrong side of bias strip; fold bias strip over piping cord. Use a zipper foot to stitch close to cord to make **piping**. Trim seam allowances to $^1/_4$".

### STRAPS

1. Center and fuse **batting straps** to wrong side of **strap linings**.
2. Cut four 28" lengths of piping. Matching raw edges, baste piping to each long edge of each **strap**.
3. Using a zipper foot, sew each strap to strap lining just inside basting. Turn straps right side out.
4. Topstitch along each edge of straps.

### BACK POCKET

1. Cut an 11" length of piping. Using a zipper foot, baste piping to 1 edge of **back pocket**.
2. Sew back pocket to **pocket cuff** (with piping sandwiched in between), stitching just inside basting.
3. Using a regular stitch length for 2"-3" at each end and a basting stitch in center, sew **back pocket lining** to pocket cuff. Press all seam allowances toward cuff.
4. Matching right sides and bottom edges, fold pocket and pocket lining together; sew along raw edges.
5. Remove basting between pocket lining and cuff. Turn pocket right side out; press. Topstitch through all layers just above piping.

### BAG FRONT

1. Centering daisy, trim **Unit 2** to $13^1/_2$" x $13^1/_2$". Sew **side**, then **top** and **bottom inner borders** to Unit 2. Sew 1 **side outer border** to each side of Unit 2. Sew **bottom outer border** to Unit 2 to make **Unit 3**.
2. Measure $4^1/_2$" from each side of Unit 3; mark. With right sides facing, pin ends of one strap to Unit 3 at marks. Baste across strap ends (Fig. 7).

**Fig. 7**

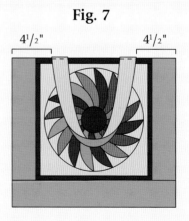

3. Sew 1 **top outer border** to Unit 3 over ends of straps, stitching through all layers. Fold border and strap up to make **bag front**; press.

**Bag Front**

4. Center **batting front** on wrong side of **front backing**. Layer bag front, right side up on batting; fuse layers together.
5. Refer to **Quilting**, page 74, to quilt as desired. The bag front is quilted in the ditch around each petal and along inner borders. The background around the daisy is stipple quilted. The outer border is echo quilted outside the inner border. Trim backing even with bag front.

## BAG BACK

1. Repeat **Bag Front**, Steps 2-4, using **bag back**, **batting back**, **back backing**, and remaining top outer border and strap.
2. Quilt as desired. The bag back is quilted with diagonal crosshatch quilting. Trim backing even with bag back.
3. Center back pocket $2^1/2$" below top edge on quilted bag back. Topstitch in place with 2 parallel lines of stitching along sides and bottom.

## BAG BOTTOM AND SIDES

1. Center 1 **side batting** on wrong side of each **side backing**. Center **bottom batting** on **bottom backing**.
2. Layer 1 **bag side**, right side up, on each side batting; fuse layers together. Quilt as desired. The bag sides are quilted around the floral print in the fabric and stipple quilted in between.
3. Repeat Steps 1-2 with bag bottom. The bottom is quilted around the floral print in the fabric.
4. Trim backing even with bag bottom and bag sides.

## INSIDE POCKETS

1. To hem top edge, press 1 long edge of **large inside pocket** $1/4$" to wrong side; press $1/2$" to wrong side. Topstitch hem in place.
2. Press remaining edges of pocket $1/4$" to wrong side.
3. Centering horizontally, pin pocket $3^3/4$" from 1 long edge of **back lining**. Topstitch pocket in place along side and bottom edges. Topstitch pocket divider lines as desired.
4. Repeat Steps 1-2 for **medium inside pocket**, hemming 1 short edge.
5. Pin pocket 3" from left edge and $2^1/2$" from top edge of back lining. Topstitch pocket in place along side and bottom edges. Topstitch pocket divider lines as desired.
6. To make casing, press 1 short edge of **small inside pocket** $1/4$" to wrong side; press $1/2$" to wrong side. To box corner, match right sides and fold bottom edge to align with 1 side edge. Measure $1^1/2$" from point and stitch from point to edges of pocket (**Fig. 8**). Repeat for remaining lower corner of pocket.

**Fig. 8**

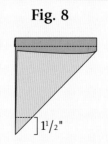

7. Insert elastic in casing. Baste ends even with side edges of pocket.
8. Press raw edges $1/4$" to wrong side.
9. Pin pocket 3" from right edge and $2^1/2$" from top edge of back lining. Topstitch pocket in place along side and bottom edges.

## BAG ASSEMBLY

1. Sew short edge of 1 bag side to each short end of bag bottom. Sew bag front to sides and bottom. Sew bag back to sides and bottom. Do not turn right side out at this time.
2. Beginning and ending behind a strap and overlapping ends (**Fig. 9**, strap not shown), baste remaining piping to top edge of bag.

**Fig. 9**

3. Sew short edge of 1 **side lining** to each short end of **bottom lining**. Sew **front lining** to sides and bottom. Leaving an opening for turning, sew **back lining** to sides and bottom.
4. Matching right sides, place lining inside bag. Using a zipper foot, sew around top edge just inside basting. Turn bag right side out. Sew opening closed. Place lining inside bag. Topstitch along top edge of bag.

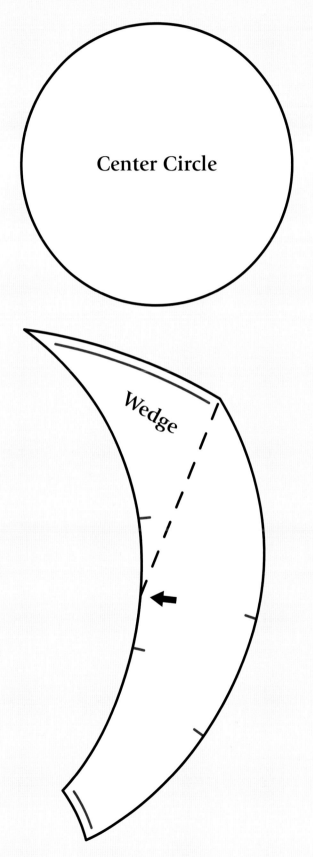

Center Circle

Wedge

# MARINER'S SWIRL

Add a nautical flair to your décor with this large Mariner's Swirl floor pillow. Inspired by a mariner's compass motif, this design puts a new spin on the traditional version with curved points creating a windblown swirl.

## FABRIC REQUIREMENTS

*Yardage is based on 43"/44" (109 cm/112 cm) wide fabric.*

$1^1/8$ yds (1 m) of cream print

$1^3/4$ yds (1.6 m) of dark blue print (includes pillow backing)

$3/8$ yd (34 cm) of blue print

$1/2$ yd (46 cm) of red print

$7/8$ yd (80 cm) of fabric for lining

*You will also need:*

Compass capable of drawing a 20"-21" (51 cm - 53 cm) circle *or* a pencil, thumbtack, and string

30" x 30" (76 cm x 76 cm) square of batting

28" x 28" (71 cm x 71 cm) pillow form

Roxanne™ Glue-Baste-It

> **TIP**
>
> To make your pillow full, like the model, use a pillow form that measures slightly larger than the finished pillow size.

## CUTTING THE PIECES

*Refer to **Making And Using Templates**, page 6, to use patterns, page 39, to make templates. When cutting out pieces, add $3/8$" – $1/2$" seam allowances to **all edges** of wedges. The Center Circle and the wedges for the Center Star will be cut later during assembly. Refer to **Rotary Cutting**, page 72, for all other cutting. All pieces given as measurements include seam allowances.*

**From cream print:**
- Cut 1 **background square** $24^1/2$" x $24^1/2$".
- Cut 16 **wedges** using template **4**.

**From dark blue print:**
- Cut 2 **side outer borders** $2^3/4$" x $23^1/2$".
- Cut 2 **top/bottom outer borders** $2^3/4$" x 28".
- Cut 2 **backs** 16" x 28".
- Cut 16 **wedges** using template **3**.

**From blue print:**
- Cut 16 **wedges** using template **1**.
- Set aside remaining fabric for Center Star.

**From red print:**
- Cut 2 **side inner borders** 1" x $22^1/2$".
- Cut 2 **top/bottom inner borders** 1" x $23^1/2$".
- Cut 16 **wedges** using template **2**.
- Set aside remaining fabric for Center Star and Center Circle.

**From lining fabric:**
- Cut 1 **lining** 30" x 30".

> **TIP**
>
> Fussy-cut wedges by centering wedge templates over the fabric motifs you wish to highlight.

## MAKING THE PILLOW TOP CENTER

*Refer to **Getting Started**, page 4, and **Practice Lesson**, page 8, for techniques. When instructed to glue and then sew wedges or Units, you will need to loosen or remove the templates of adjoining wedges, sew the seam, and then re-attach the templates.*

> *Note: Our Figs. and Diagrams are shown without templates and seam allowances. Your wedges will have templates attached and seam allowances showing.*

### OUTER SWIRL

1. Press under the *concave* Step 1 edge of **wedge 2**. Glue and then sew **wedge 1** and wedge 2 together to make **Unit 1**.

**Unit 1**

2. Press under the *concave* Step 1 edge of **wedge 3**. Glue and then sew wedge 3 and Unit 1 together to make **Unit 2**.

**Unit 2**

3. Press under the *concave* Step 1 edge of **wedge 4**. Glue and then sew wedge 4 and Unit 2 together to make **Unit 3**. Make 16 Unit 3's.

**Unit 3 (make 16)**

4. Press under the *concave* Step 2 edge of each Unit 3. Aligning seams (**Fig. 1**), glue and then sew Unit 3's together to make **Outer Swirl**. Use water-soluble fabric marker or wash-out pencil to draw around templates onto the seam allowances of each wedge where indicated by dark pink lines on templates. Remove templates.

**Fig. 1**          **Outer Swirl**

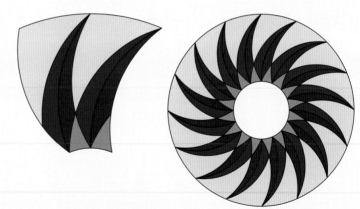

## BACKGROUND

1. Measure across the center of the outer swirl from outer drawn line to outer drawn line in 3 places (**Fig. 2**). From these measurements, determine **average diameter**. Divide average diameter by 2 to determine **radius**. For example, the average diameter of **Fig. 2** is 20$\frac{1}{2}$", so the radius is 10$\frac{1}{4}$".

**Fig. 2**

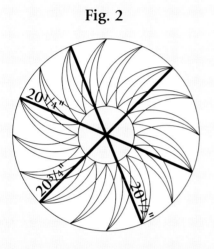

2. To make a background template, refer to **Working With Freezer Paper**, page 6, to join pieces of freezer paper to make a single piece large enough to cut a 22" x 22" square.
3. Fold freezer paper square in half horizontally and vertically and mark center; unfold.
4. Placing point of compass on center mark, draw a circle using determined radius. *Note:* To make a compass, tie a length of string to a pencil. Insert a thumbtack in the string at determined radius. Place thumbtack through center mark of freezer paper square. Holding string taut, draw a circle.

> **TIP**
> The diameter of the drawn circle should measure the same as the average diameter determined in Step 1.

5. Cut out circle on drawn line; discard circle. The remaining square is your background template. Aligning center opening of background template with drawn line of outer swirl, place template over outer swirl to check size (**Fig. 3**).

**Fig. 3**

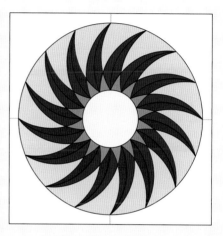

6. If opening of template is too small and points of swirl are cut off, trim opening to the size needed. If opening is too big, repeat Steps 1-5 to re-measure outer swirl and cut another template.
7. Fold **background square** in half horizontally and vertically and crease; unfold.

8. Aligning crease lines, press background template onto right side of background square (**Fig. 4**).

**Fig. 4**

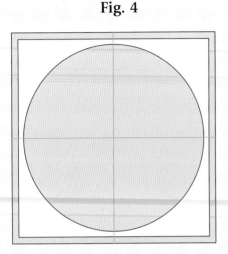

9. Using inner edge of template as a guide and leaving a $^3/_8$" to $^1/_2$" seam allowance, cut out center of background square.

10. With template side down and clipping as needed, press seam allowance to the wrong side around opening (**Fig. 5**).

**Fig. 5**

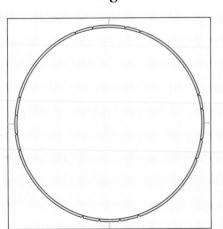

11. Referring to **Unit 4 Diagram**, match crease lines of background square with points of outer swirl and align pressed edge of background square with drawn line of outer swirl. *Note:* Every 4th point should align with a crease line on background square.

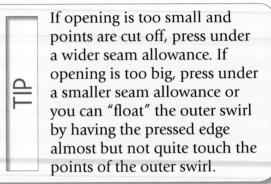

TIP

If opening is too small and points are cut off, press under a wider seam allowance. If opening is too big, press under a smaller seam allowance or you can "float" the outer swirl by having the pressed edge almost but not quite touch the points of the outer swirl.

12. When satisfied with opening size and placement, glue and then sew background square and outer swirl together to make **Unit 4**. Remove background template.

**Unit 4**

## CENTER STAR

1. Measure across the center opening of Unit 4 from inner drawn line to inner drawn line in 3 places (**Fig. 6**).

**Fig. 6**

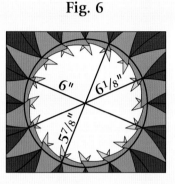

2. If your measurement is 6", continue with Step 3, below. If your measurement is larger or smaller than 6", enlarge or reduce the **Center Star** pattern, page 39, to equal your measurement, then continue with Step 3.

3. Tracing only the outer line of the Center Star pattern, trace and cut out an outer circle template. Set template aside.

4. Tracing the entire pattern, make a freezer paper template from Center Star pattern; cut template apart on traced lines.

5. Cut the following pieces:
   **From blue print:**
   • Cut 8 **wedges** using template 5.
   **From red print:**
   • Cut 8 **wedges** using template 6.
   • Cut 1 **center circle** using template 7.

6. Press under the Step 1 edge of **wedge 5**. Glue and then sew wedge 5 and **wedge 6** together to make **Unit 5**. Make 8 Unit 5's.

**Unit 5** (make 8)

7. Press under the Step 2 edge of each Unit 5. Glue and then sew Unit 5's together to make **Unit 6**. Remove templates.

**Unit 6**

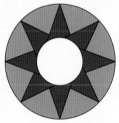

8. Refer to **Attaching the Center Oval Or Circle**, Steps 2-3, page 12, to attach **center circle** to Unit 6 to make **Center Star**. Using your preferred method, **Appliqué**, page 73, the center circle in place.

9. Center and press outer circle template onto Center Star. Attach Center Star to center of Unit 4 to make **Pillow Top Center**. Using your preferred method, **Appliqué**, page 73, the Center Star to Unit 4. Square pillow top center to $22^1/_2$" x $22^1/_2$".

**Pillow Top Center**

## ASSEMBLING THE PILLOW

*Match right sides and use a $^1/_4$" seam allowance unless otherwise noted.*

1. Sew **side**, then **top/bottom inner borders** to pillow top center.
2. Sew **side**, then **top/bottom outer borders** to pillow top to make **Pillow Front**.

**Pillow Front**

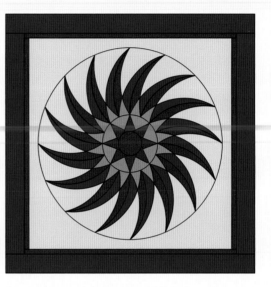

3. Refer to **Quilting**, page 74, to mark, layer and quilt pillow front, **batting** and **lining** as desired. The model is quilted in the ditch between the borders and between the inner border and background. Each point of the outer swirl and around the outer edge of the background is echo quilted with quilting lines spaced approximately $^1/_2$" apart. There is outline quilting around the blue print wedges and center circle.
4. Trim batting and lining even with pillow top.
5. Press 1 long edge of each **back** $^1/_4$" to the wrong side twice. Topstitch hem close to the folded edges.
6. With right sides facing up, overlap the two hemmed edges of the pillow backs until the overall measurement is 28" x 28". Baste the overlapped edges together.
7. Using a $^1/_2$" seam allowance, sew pillow front and back together to make **Pillow**. Clip corners and turn right side out. Topstitch around pillow $^1/_2$" from outer edges. Insert pillow form.

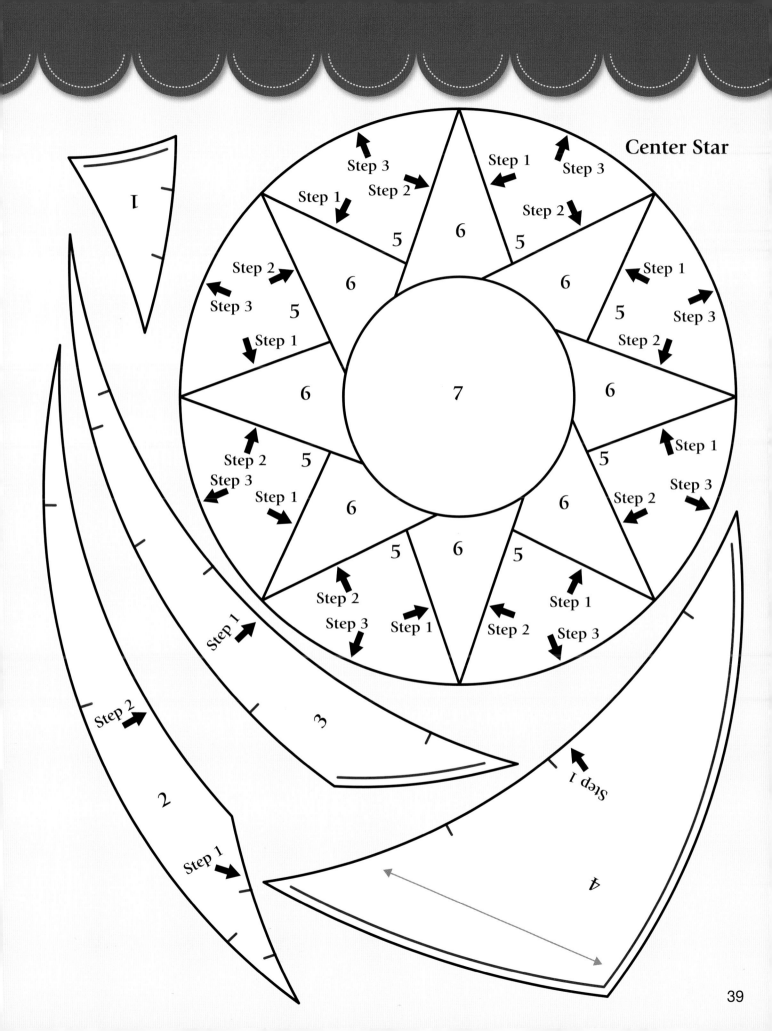

Center Star

39

*Each black or white corner unit of this fun wall hanging can be cut from an 8" square of fabric. If you are thinking scrappy and need to purchase fabric, you may consider buying a 10" square Layer Cake bundle. Add in a little yardage for the red "ribbons" and binding and this merry quilt could be dancing on your wall in no time!*

## FABRIC REQUIREMENTS
*Yardage is based on 43"/44" (109 cm/112 cm) wide fabric.*
   1 Layer Cake *or* 18 squares 8" x 8" (20 cm x 20 cm)
      *each* of assorted black prints *and* assorted white
      prints
   1¼ yds (1.1 m) of red print
   1¼ yds (1.1 m) of fabric for backing
*You will also need:*
   40" x 40" (102 cm x 102 cm) square of batting
   Roxanne™ Glue-Baste-It

## CUTTING THE PIECES
*Refer to **Making And Using Templates**, page 6, to use patterns, page 45, to make templates. When cutting out pieces, add ³⁄₈" – ¹⁄₂" seam allowances to **all edges** of wedges and ribbons. Refer to **Rotary Cutting**, page 72, for all other cutting.*

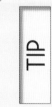

TIP

When cutting, place 1 set of ribbons with each set of wedges. To keep sets together, fold sheets of ready-to-be-recycled paper into "envelopes" for each set and place them in a small box to carry from your cutting area to your sewing area.

**From black prints:**
   • Cut 18 *sets* of **wedges** using templates **1**, **4**, and **5**.
**From white prints:**
   • Cut 18 *sets* of **wedges** using templates **1**, **4**, and **5**.
**From red print:**
   • Cut 1 **binding square** 20" x 20".
   • Cut 36 *sets* of **ribbons** using templates **2** and **3**.
**From backing fabric:**
   • Cut 1 **backing square** 40" x 40".

## MAKING THE BLOCKS
*Refer to **Getting Started**, page 4, and **Practice Lesson**, page 8, for techniques. When instructed to glue and then sew wedges or Units, you will need to loosen or remove the templates of adjoining wedges or Units, sew the seam, and then re-attach the templates.*

*Note: Figs. and Diagrams are shown without templates but the seam allowances are shown and the seamlines are indicated by the grey lines. Your wedges will have templates attached.*

1.  Select 1 set of wedges and ribbons. Press under the Step 1 *concave* edge of **wedges 1**, **4**, and **5**.
2.  Glue and then sew wedge 1 and **ribbon 2** together to make **Unit 1**.

### Unit 1

3.  Glue and then sew wedge 4 and **ribbon 3** together to make **Unit 2**.

### Unit 2

41

4. Press under the Step 1 *concave* edge of Unit 2. Glue and then sew Units 1 and 2 together to make **Unit 3**.

**Unit 3**

5. Press under the Step 1 *concave* edge of Unit 3. Glue and then sew Unit 3 and wedge 5 together to make **Corner Unit**. Make 36 Corner Units.

**Corner Unit** (make 36)

6. Press under the Step 2 *concave* edge of each Corner Unit.

7. Use water-soluble fabric marker or wash-out pencil to draw around templates where indicated onto each Corner Unit (**Fig.1**). Mark dots on the seam allowance at each corner where indicated by triangles on templates as shown; remove templates.

**Fig. 1**

8. Select 1 white and 1 black Corner Unit. Align ribbons and marked dots to glue and then sew Corner Units together to make **Unit 4**. Make 18 Unit 4's.

**Unit 4** (make 18)

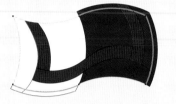

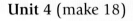

TIP

To speed production and stay organized, always place a white Corner Block on the left when making Unit 4's.

9. For Block, select 2 Unit 4's. Rotate Unit 4's to place white and black fabrics opposite each other (**Fig. 2**).

**Fig. 2**

**10.** Working on half of a Unit 4 at a time, align ribbons and marked dots to glue the 2 Unit 4's together (**Fig. 3**). Glue remaining half of Units together. When viewed from the wrong side, seam allowances will nest opposite each other (**Fig. 4**).

**11.** Starting and stopping exactly on marked dot and keeping seam allowances out of stitching, sew half of glued seam (**Fig. 5**). Repeat to sew remaining half of glued seam together to make **Block**. Make 9 Blocks.

Fig. 3

Fig. 5

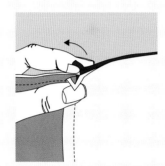

Fig. 4

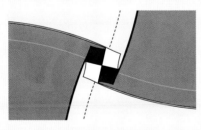

**Block** (make 9)

## ASSEMBLING THE QUILT TOP

1. To check fabric and color placement, arrange Blocks into 3 horizontal rows of 3 Blocks each.
2. Turn Blocks wrong side up. Before sewing Blocks together, clip seam allowances up to but not through the stitching in the center of the red ribbons. Press the seam allowances as shown in **Fig. 6**.

**Fig. 6**

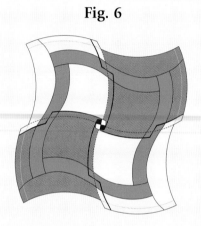

3. Working on half of a Block at a time, in the same manner as **Making the Blocks**, Steps 10 – 11, match marked dots to glue and sew 2 Blocks together. Glue and sew remaining half of Block. When viewed from the wrong side, seam allowances will nest opposite each other and the sharp points of fabric will fold away from center (**Fig. 7**). In same manner, add a third Block to make a **Row**. Make 3 Rows.

**Fig. 7**

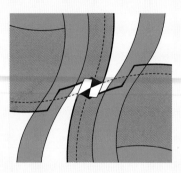

Row (make 3)

4. Using same technique used to glue and sew Blocks into Rows, glue and sew Rows together to make **Quilt Top**.

## FINISHING

1.  Press open all exterior seam allowances.
2.  Refer to **Quilting**, page 74, to mark, layer, and quilt as desired. The model is outline quilted around each wedge. There is a line quilted through the center of each red ribbon and an echo of the ribbon shape in the center of each Block.

3.  Use binding square and follow **Making A Continuous Bias Strip**, page 77, to make 2$^1/_4$"w bias binding. Follow **Attaching Binding with Mitered Corners**, page 78, to bind quilt.

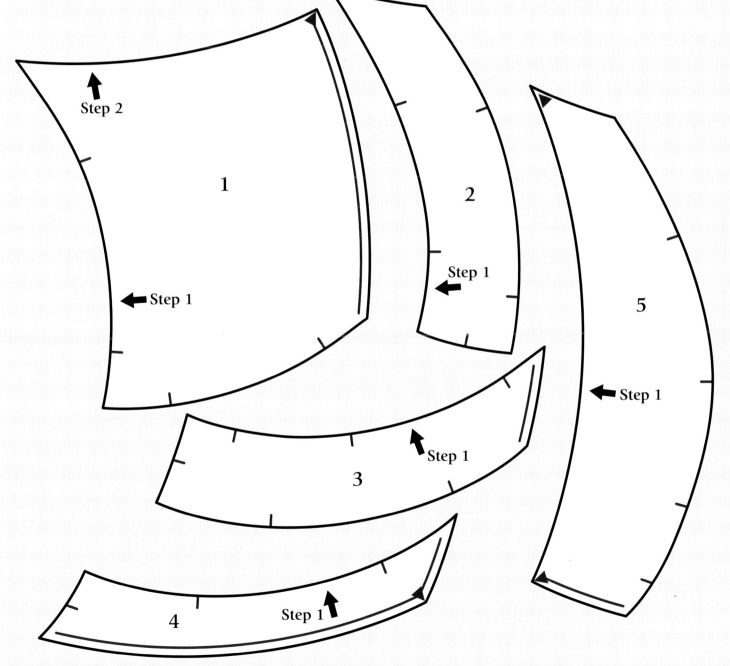

# CELTIC KNOT TABLE RUNNER

Brighten your home with this lovely Celtic Knot Table Runner. This design, as typical of Celtic knots and braids, has no visible beginning or end. Thought to represent endless love, the eternity of nature, and the uninterrupted cycle of life, Celtic knots are often considered symbols of longevity or good luck with new endeavors.

## FABRIC REQUIREMENTS

*Yardage is based on 43"/44" (109 cm/112 cm) wide fabric.*

$1/2$ yd (57 cm) of blue print

$3/4$ yd (69 cm) of blue/yellow print

$1 1/4$ yds (1.1 m) of yellow/white print

19" x 19" (48 cm x 48 cm) square of yellow solid (binding)

$1 3/8$ yds (1.3 m) of fabric for backing

*You will also need:*

$3 1/2$ yds (3.2 m) of $1/8$" (3 mm) diameter piping cord

47" x 29" (119 cm x 74 cm) rectangle of batting

Roxanne™ Glue-Baste-It

## CUTTING THE PIECES

*Refer to **Making And Using Templates**, page 6, to use patterns, pages 51-61, to make templates. Each wedge A-D is made up of 7 sub-wedges with the wedge letter and a number 1-7. When cutting out pieces, add $3/8$" – $1/2$" seam allowances to all **curved edges** of sub-wedges and outer oval. Add a $1/4$" seam allowance to **center oval**. Refer to Rotary Cutting, page 72, for all other cutting.*

**From blue print:**
- Cut 2 **sub-wedges** from *each* template **A-4**, **B-2**, **B-7**, **C-4**, **D-2**, and **D-7**.

**From blue/yellow print:**
- Cut 2 **sub-wedges** from *each* template **A-2**, **A-7**, **B-4**, **C-2**, **C-7**, and **D-4**.
- Cut 1 **piping square** 18" x 18".

**From yellow/white print:**
- Cut 2 **sub-wedges** from *each* template **A-1**, **A-3**, **A-5**, and **A-6**.
- Cut 2 **sub-wedges** from *each* template **B-1**, **B-3**, **B-5**, and **B-6**.
- Cut 2 **sub-wedges** from *each* template **C-1**, **C-3**, **C-5**, and **C-6**.
- Cut 2 **sub-wedges** from *each* template **D-1**, **D-3**, **D-5**, and **D-6**.
- Cut 1 **center oval**.
- Cut 2 **outer ovals** and 2 **outer ovals in reverse**.

**From backing fabric:**
- Cut 1 **backing** 47" x 29".

## MAKING THE TABLE RUNNER TOP

*Refer to **Getting Started**, page 4, and **Practice Lesson**, page 8, for techniques. When instructed to glue and then sew wedges or Units, you will need to glue seam, loosen or remove the templates of adjoining wedges, sew the seam, and then re-attach the templates.*

*Note: Our Figs. and Diagrams are shown without templates and seam allowances. Your sub-wedges will have templates attached and seam allowances showing. Referring to template markings, note that some registration marks will align with seams in adjoining wedges.*

### TABLE RUNNER CENTER

1. Referring to **Wedge A Diagram**, page 48, arrange **sub-wedges A-1 – A-7** into 2 Wedge A shapes.
2. Press under the Step 1 *concave* edge of **sub-wedges A-2, A-3** and **A-4**. Glue and then sew sub-wedges A-2 – A-5 together to make **Unit 1**. Make 2 Unit 1's.

**Unit 1** (make 2)

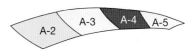

3. Press under the Step 1 *concave* edge of **sub-wedge A-7**. Glue and then sew sub-wedge A-7 and sub-wedge **A-6** together to make **Unit 2**. Make 2 Unit 2's.

**Unit 2** (make 2)

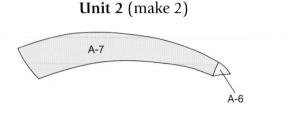

4. Press under the Step 2 *concave* edge of **Unit 2**. Glue and then sew Units 1 and 2 together to make **Unit 3**. Make 2 Unit 3's.

**Unit 3** (make 2)

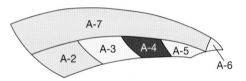

5. Press under the Step 1 *concave* edge of **sub-wedge A-1**. Glue and then sew sub-wedge A-1 and Unit 3 together to make **Wedge A**. Make 2 Wedge A's.

**Wedge A** (make 2)

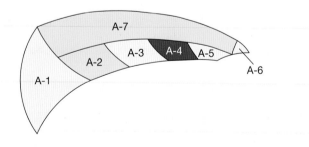

6. Repeat Steps 1-5 using sub-wedges **B-1 – B-7** to make 2 **Wedge B's**, sub-wedges **C-1 – C-7** to make 2 **Wedge C's**, and sub-wedges **D-1 – D-7** to make 2 **Wedge D's**.

**Wedge B** (make 2)

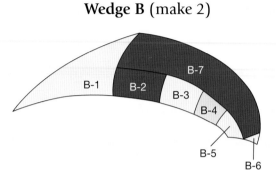

**Wedge C** (make 2)

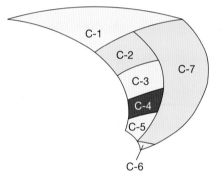

**Wedge D** (make 2)

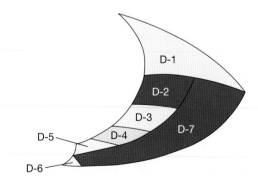

7. Press under the long *concave* edge of 1 wedge B. Aligning seams of wedge B with registration marks of 1 wedge A, glue and then sew wedges together to make **Unit 4**. Make 2 Unit 4's.

**Unit 4** (make 2)

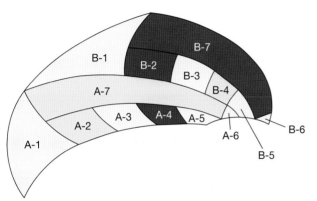

8. Press under the long *concave* edge of 1 wedge D. Aligning seams of wedge D with registration marks of wedge C, glue and then sew wedges together to make **Unit 5**. Make 2 Unit 5's.

**Unit 5** (make 2)

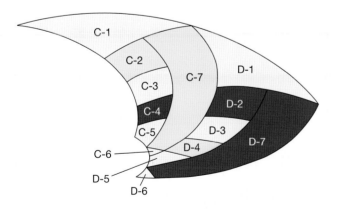

9. Press under the long *concave* edge of each Unit 5. Aligning seams and registration marks, glue and then sew 1 Unit 4 and 1 Unit 5 together to make **Unit 6**. Make 2 Unit 6's.

**Unit 6** (make 2)

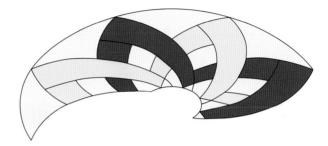

10. Press under the long *concave* edge of each Unit 6. Aligning seams and registration marks, glue and then sew 2 Unit 6's together to make **Table Runner Center**.

11. Referring to **Attaching The Center Oval Or Circle**, Steps 2-3, page 12, attach **center oval** to the center of table runner center. Using your preferred method, **Appliqué**, page 73, the center oval in place.

**Table Runner Center**

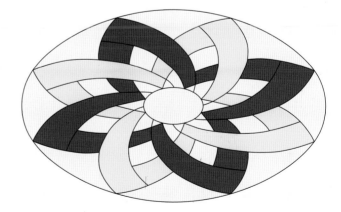

12. Using center side and top/bottom registration marks on template as a guide, mark the center side and top/bottom of the table runner center. Remove templates.

49

## BACKGROUND OVAL

1. Loosen templates at each straight edge of each Outer Oval and Outer Oval reversed; fold or pin templates out of the way. Using a $1/4$" seam allowance, match right sides and sew 1 Outer Oval and 1 Outer Oval reversed together to make half Background Oval; repeat. Sew two halves together to make **Background Oval**. Re-attach templates.

**Background Oval**

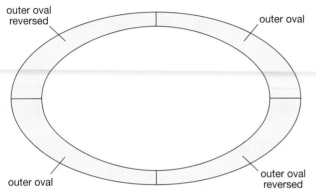

2. With template side facing down and clipping as needed, press seam allowance to the wrong side around opening (**Fig. 1**).

**Fig. 1**

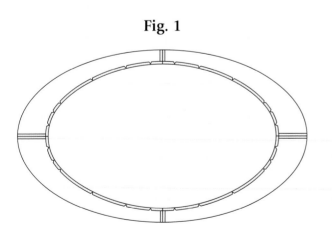

3. Referring to **Table Runner Top Diagram** and matching seams of background oval with marks on sides and top/bottom of table runner center, place background oval over table runner center to check placement.

> **TIP**
> If opening is too small and points are cut off, press under a wider seam allowance. If opening is too big, press under a smaller seam allowance or you can "float" the table runner center by having the pressed edge almost but not quite touch the points of the table runner center.

4. When satisfied with opening size and placement, glue and then sew background oval and table runner center together to make **Table Runner Top**. Remove templates.

**Table Runner Top**

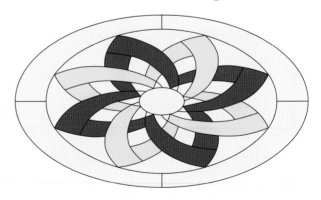

## FINISHING

1. Refer to **Quilting**, page 74, to mark, layer, and quilt table runner top as desired. Both the blue and yellow sections of the Celtic Knot and the yellow/white background fabric wedges of the model are outline quilted. There are two lines of echo quilting around the outer edges of the entire knot. The center oval is quilted with a star. The star is filled with stipple quilting. The remainder of the table runner is meander quilted.

2. Use **piping square** and follow **Making A Continuous Bias Strip**, page 77, Steps 1–7, to make approximately $3^1/2$ yds of $1^1/4$" wide **bias strip**.

3. Lay **piping cord** in center of wrong side of bias strip; fold bias strip over piping cord. Use a zipper foot to stitch close to cord to make **piping**. Trim seam allowances to $^1/4$".

4. Matching raw edges and clipping the seam allowance of the piping as needed to ease around curves, use zipper foot to baste piping to the right side of the table runner. When you reach the starting point, overlap the beginning end of the piping as shown in **Fig. 3** and continue stitching.

**Fig. 3**

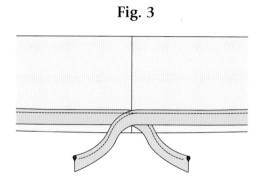

5. Use **binding square** and refer to **Making A Continuous Bias Strip**, page 77, to make $2^1/4$"w bias binding. Refer to **Attaching Binding (Celtic Knot)** page 80, to bind Table Runner.

> **TIP**
> To stitch as close as possible to the piping, use zipper foot to attach binding.

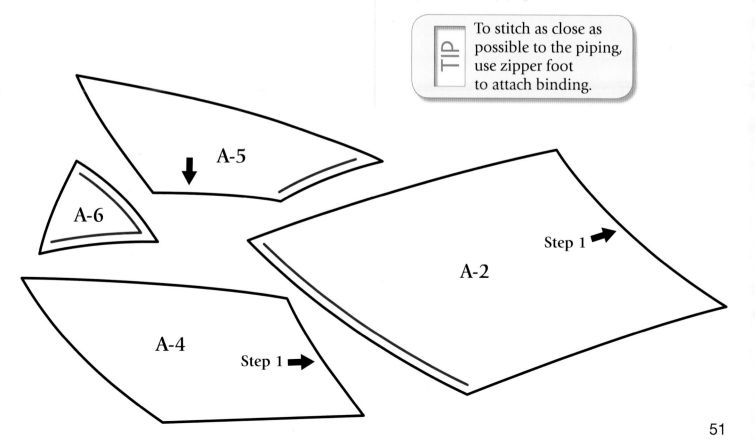

51

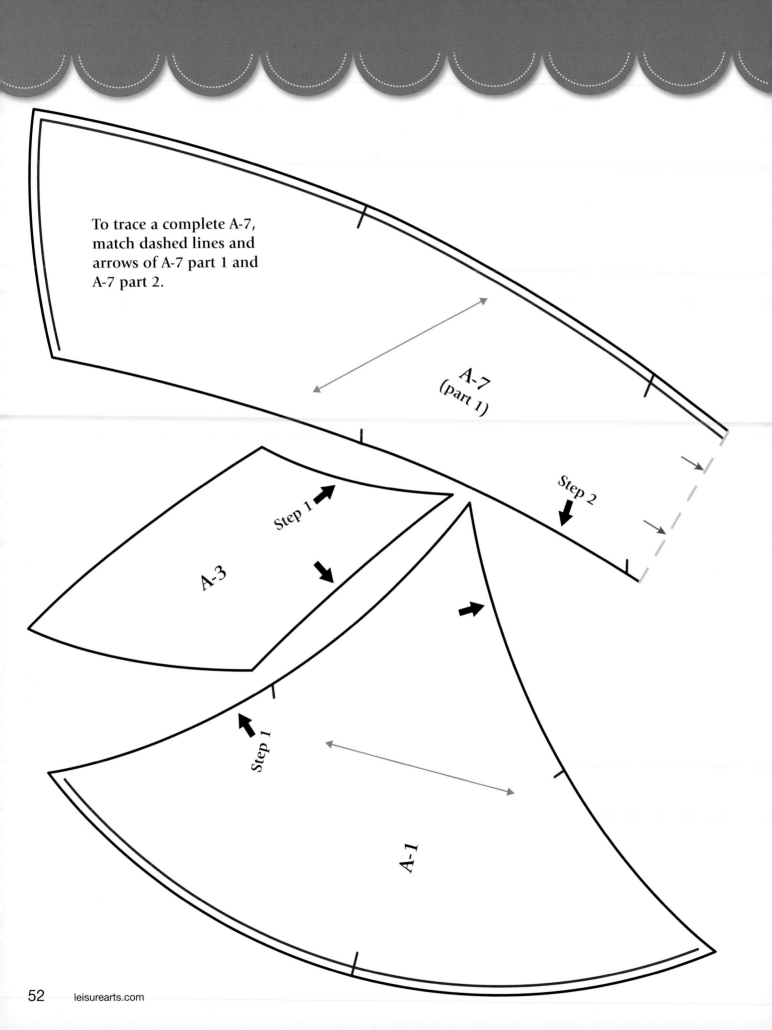

To trace a complete A-7,
match dashed lines and
arrows of A-7 part 1 and
A-7 part 2.

A-7
(part 1)

Step 2

A-3

Step 1

A-1

Step 1

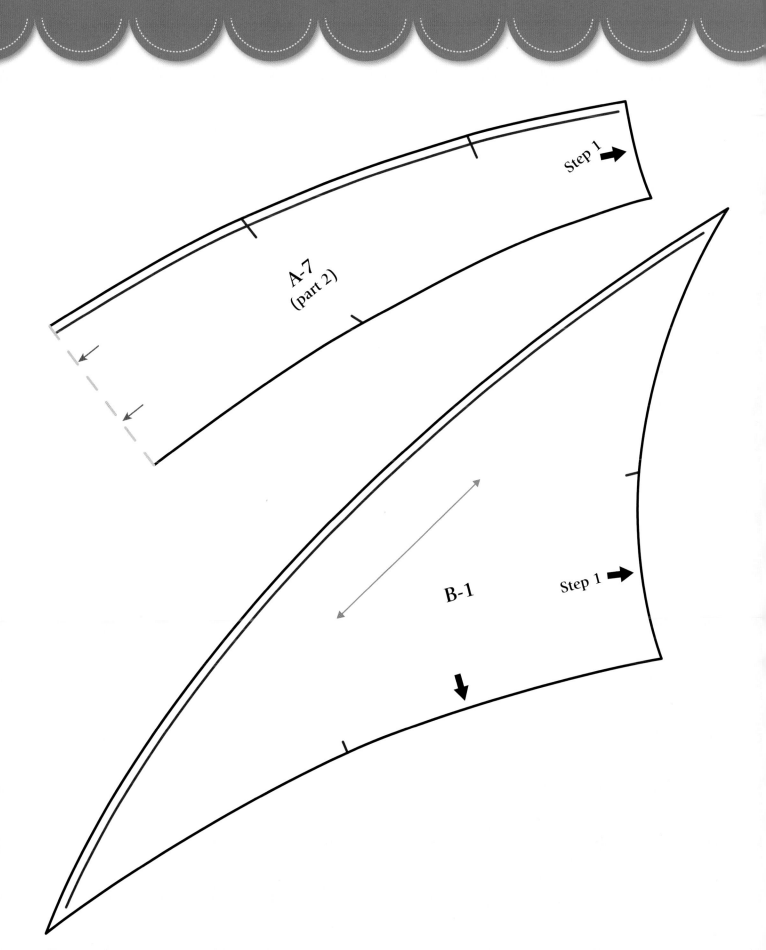

A-7
(part 2)

Step 1 →

B-1

Step 1 →

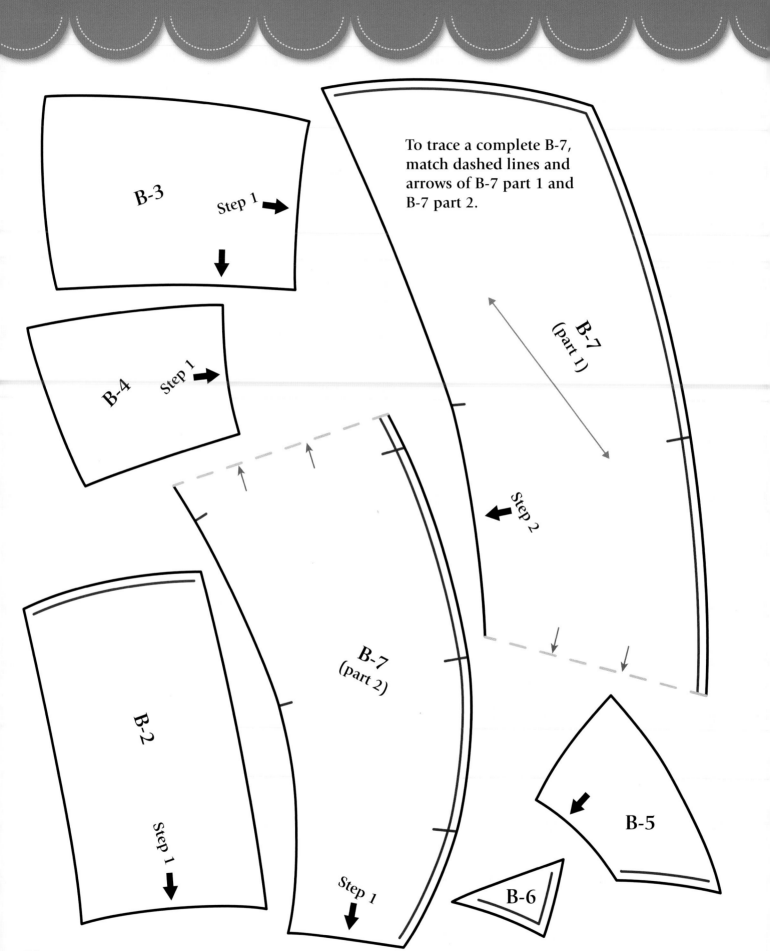

B-3

Step 1 →

B-4    Step 1 →

To trace a complete B-7, match dashed lines and arrows of B-7 part 1 and B-7 part 2.

B-7 (part 1)

← Step 2

B-7 (part 2)

B-2

Step 1

Step 1

B-5

B-6

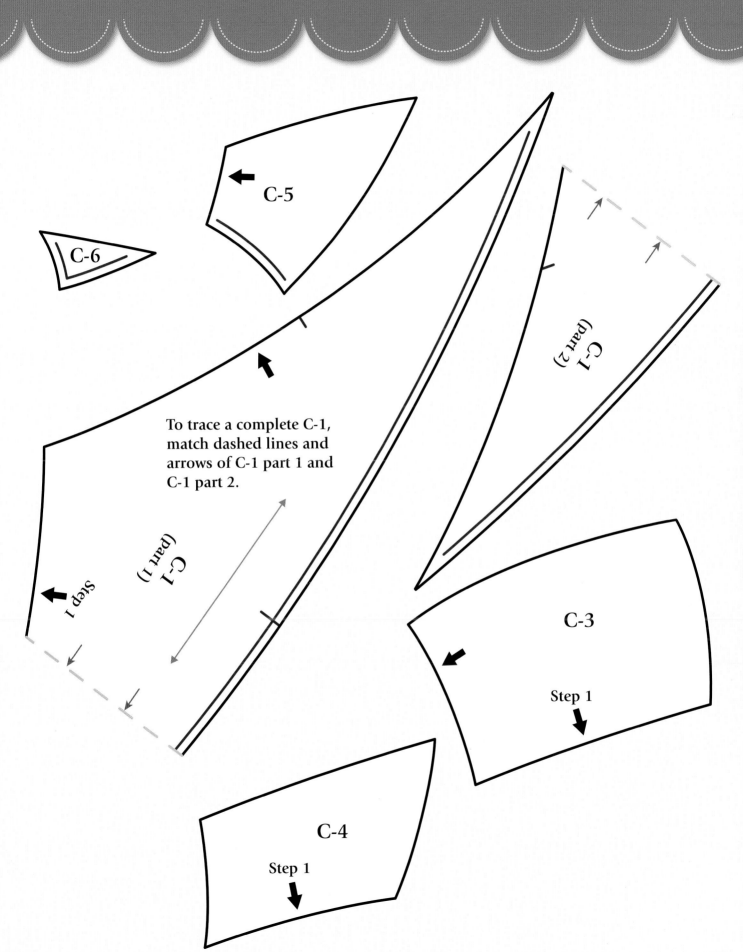

C-5

C-6

C-1 (part 2)

To trace a complete C-1, match dashed lines and arrows of C-1 part 1 and C-1 part 2.

C-1 (part 1)

Step 1

C-3

Step 1

C-4

Step 1

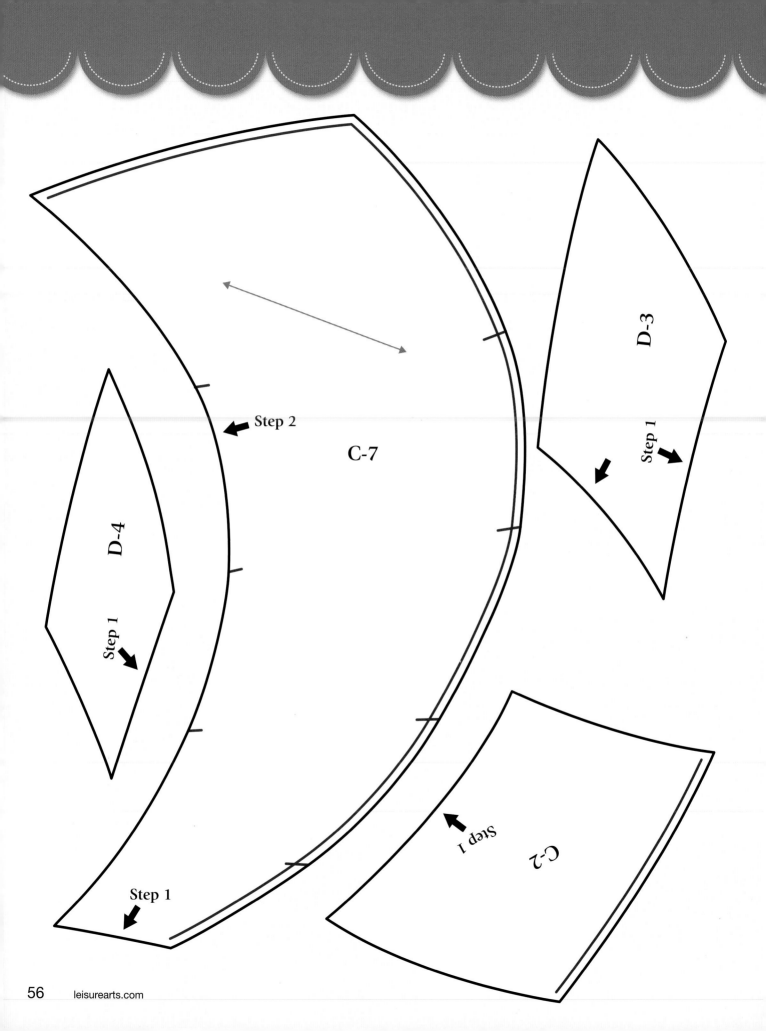

D-3

Step 1

C-7

Step 2

D-4

Step 1

Step 1

C-2

Step 1

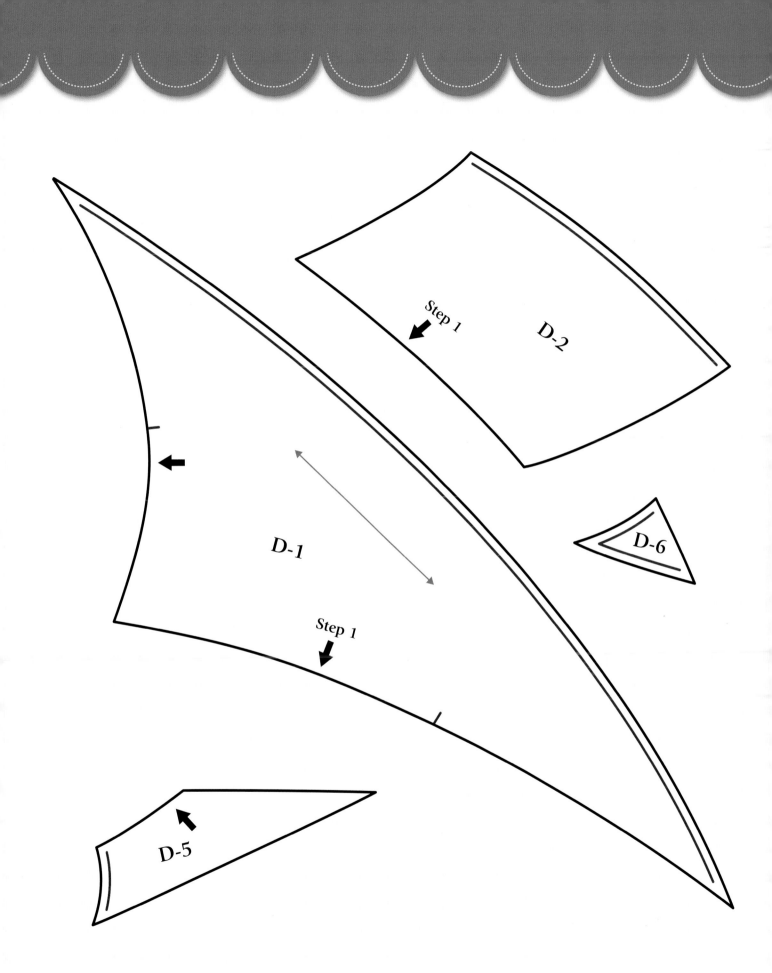

Step 1

D-2

D-6

D-1

Step 1

D-5

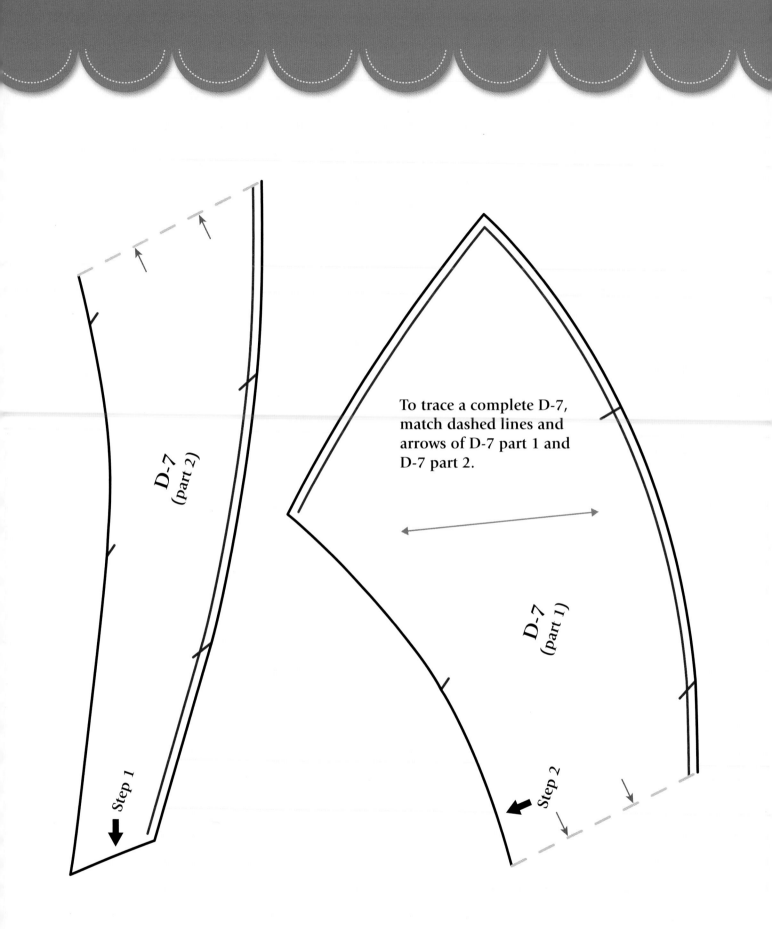

D-7
(Part 2)

D-7
(Part 1)

Step 1

Step 2

To trace a complete D-7,
match dashed lines and
arrows of D-7 part 1 and
D-7 part 2.

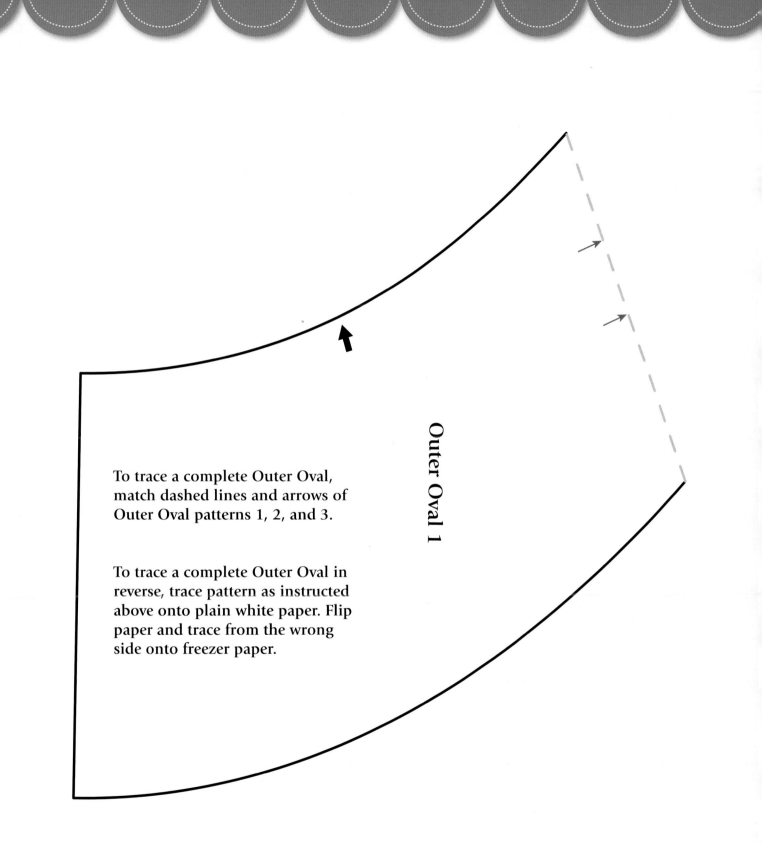

Outer Oval 1

To trace a complete Outer Oval, match dashed lines and arrows of Outer Oval patterns 1, 2, and 3.

To trace a complete Outer Oval in reverse, trace pattern as instructed above onto plain white paper. Flip paper and trace from the wrong side onto freezer paper.

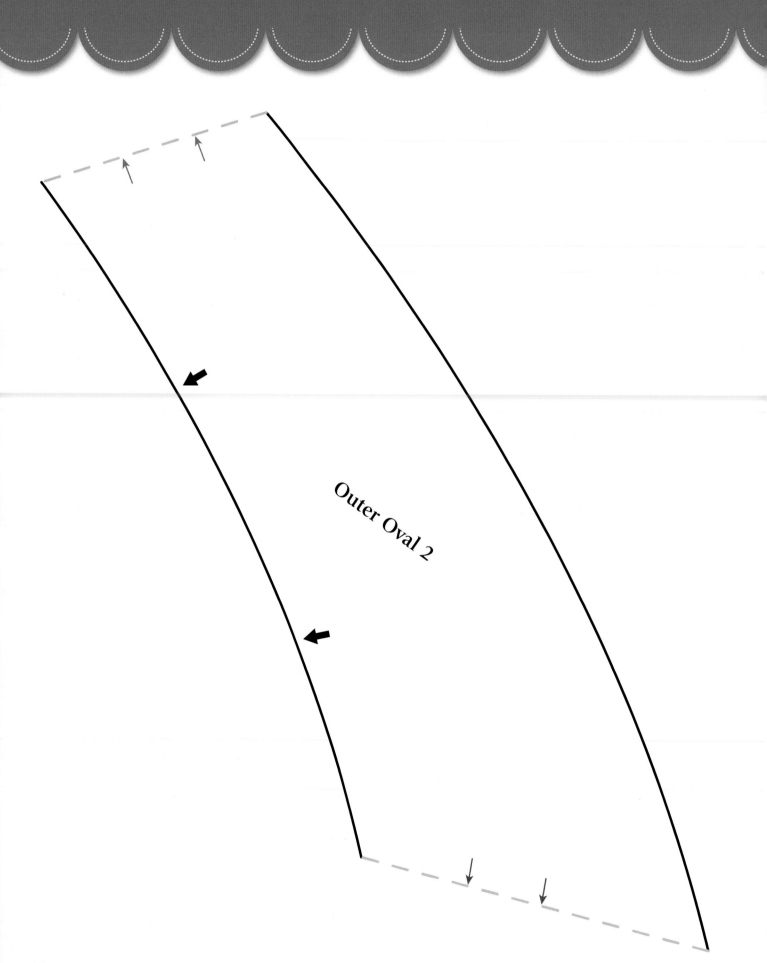

Outer Oval 2

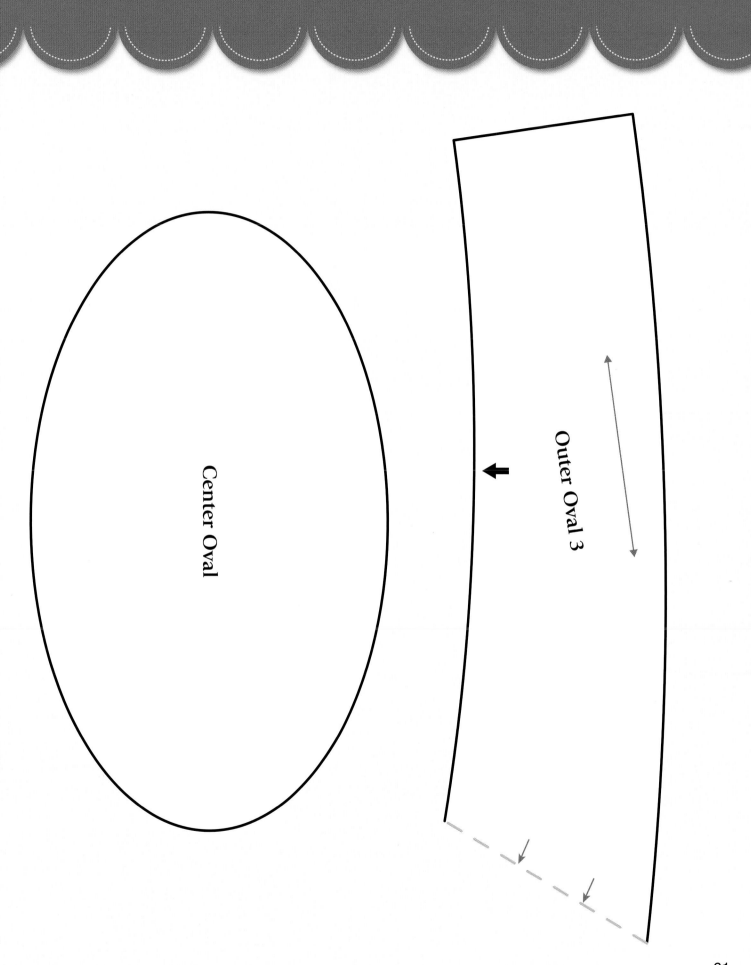

Center Oval

Outer Oval 3

This sun-drenched Spinning Cartwheel quilt is based on the traditional Giant Dahlia pattern. For extra visual interest, the petals are "split" by cutting the wedges from strip sets. The center motif, which uses the curved piecing technique, is framed by a pieced diamond border.

## FABRIC REQUIREMENTS

*Yardage is based on 43"/44" (109 cm/112 cm) wide fabric.*

$1^3/_4$ yds (1.6 m) of cream print

$^1/_2$ yd (46 cm) *each* of 3 pink prints

$1^1/_4$ yds (1.1 m) of pink print #4 (includes binding)

$^1/_2$ yd (46 cm) of pink dot

$^1/_2$ yd (46 cm) *each* of 4 orange prints

$1^5/_8$ yds (1.5 m) of yellow polka dot

$3^3/_8$ yds (3.1 m) of fabric for backing

*You will also need:*

Compass capable of drawing a 30"–31" circle *or* a pencil, thumbtack, and string

60" x 60" (152 cm x 152 cm) square of batting

Roxanne™ Glue-Baste-It

## CUTTING THE PIECES

*Refer to **Making And Using Templates**, page 6, to use patterns, pages 70-71. When cutting out pieces, add $^3/_8$" – $^1/_2$" seam allowances to all **curved edges** of sub-wedges. Add a $^1/_4$" seam allowance to **center circle**. Add an accurate $^1/_4$" seam allowance to all **edges** of diamonds, medium triangles, and large triangles. Refer to **Rotary Cutting**, page 72, for all other cutting. Borders are cut exact length and all pieces given as measurements include seam allowances.*

**From cream print:**
- Cut 1 **background square** $36^1/_2$" x $36^1/_2$".
- Cut 16 **sub-wedges** using template **E**.
- Cut 16 **sub-wedges** using template **F**.
- Cut 8 **medium triangles** and 4 **medium triangles in reverse** using template **G**.
- Cut 24 **large triangles** using template **H**.
- Cut 1 **center circle**.
- Cut 2 **squares** 3" x 3". Cut squares once diagonally to make 4 **small triangles**.

**From *each* of 3 pink prints:**
- Cut 4 **strips** 4" wide x width of fabric.

**From pink print #4:**
- Cut 4 **strips** 4" wide x width of fabric.
- Cut 1 **binding square** 25" x 25".
- Cut 4 **squares** $3^1/_4$" x $3^1/_4$".

**From pink dot:**
- Cut 28 **diamonds** using template **I**.

**From *each* orange print:**
- Cut 4 **strips** 4" wide x width of fabric.

**From yellow polka dot fabric:**
- Cut 2 *lengthwise* **side outer borders** $4^1/_2$" x $43^1/_2$".
- Cut 2 *lengthwise* **top/bottom outer borders** $4^1/_2$" x $51^1/_2$".
- Cut 6 **squares** 3" x 3". Cut squares once diagonally to make 12 **small triangles**.
- Cut 4 **medium triangles** and 4 **medium triangles in reverse** using template **G**.
- Cut 24 **large triangles** using template **H**.

**From freezer paper:**
- Cut 16 sets of **sub-wedge templates** using patterns 1 – 7, pages 70-71.

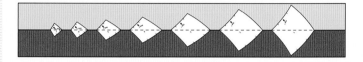

## MAKING THE QUILT TOP CENTER

*Refer to **Getting Started**, page 4, and **Practice Lesson**, page 8, for techniques. When instructed to glue and then sew wedges or Units, you will need to loosen or remove the templates of adjoining wedges, sew the seam, and then re-attach the templates.*

*Note: Our Figs. and Diagrams are shown without templates and seam allowances. Your wedges will have templates attached and seam allowances showing.*

### WEDGES

1. Select 4 like fabric pink print and 4 like fabric orange print **strips**.
2. Matching long edges and using a $^1/_4$" seam allowance, sew 1 pink and 1 orange strip together to make **Strip Set A**. Press seam allowances open. Make 4 Strip Set A's.

**Strip Set A (make 4)**

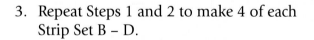

3. Repeat Steps 1 and 2 to make 4 of each Strip Set B – D.

**Strip Set B (make 4)**

**Strip Set C (make 4)**

**Strip Set D (make 4)**

4. Referring to **Cutting Diagram** and leaving at least 1" between **sub-wedge templates**, align dashed lines on templates with seam in Strip Sets to cut sub-wedges. Cut 1 set of sub-wedges **1 – 7** from each Strip Set. You will have 4 sets of sub-wedges cut from Strip Sets A to make 4 Wedge A's. You will have 4 sets of sub-wedges cut from Strip Sets B to make 4 Wedge B's, and so on.

### Cutting Diagram

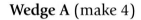

5. For wedge A, select 1 set of sub-wedges 1 – 7, 1 sub-wedge E, and 1 sub-wedge F. Press under the Step 1 *concave* edge of each sub-wedge. Glue and then sew sub-wedges together to make **Wedge A**. Make 4 Wedge A's.

**Wedge A (make 4)**

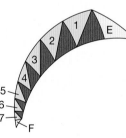

6. Repeat Step 5 to make 4 of each **Wedge B – D**.

**Wedge B (make 4)**      **Wedge C (make 4)**

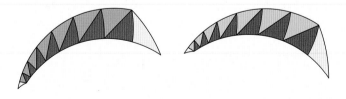

**Wedge D (make 4)**

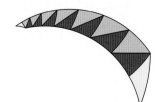

## CARTWHEEL

1. Press under the long *concave* edge of *each* **wedge** A. Aligning seamlines, glue and then sew 1 wedge A and 1 wedge B together to make **Unit 1**. Make 4 Unit 1's.

**Unit 1** (make 4)

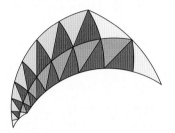

2. Press under the long *concave* edge of *each* **wedge** C. Aligning seamlines, glue and then sew 1 wedge C and 1 wedge D together to make **Unit 2**. Make 4 Unit 2's.

**Unit 2** (make 4)

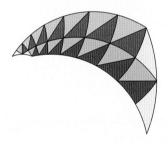

3. Press under the long *concave* edge of *each* **Unit 1**. Aligning seamlines, glue and then sew 1 Unit 1 and 1 Unit 2 together to make **Unit 3**. Make 4 Unit 3's.

**Unit 3** (make 4)

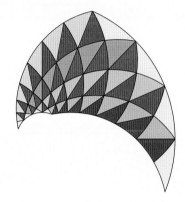

4. Press under the long *concave* edge of each Unit 3. Aligning seamlines, glue and then sew 2 Unit 3's together to make **Unit 4.** Make 2 Unit 4's.

**Unit 4** (make 2)

5. Press under the long *concave* edge of each Unit 4. Aligning seamlines, glue and then sew Unit 4's together to make **Cartwheel.** Using water-soluble marker or wash-out fabric pencil, draw around templates at inner and outer edges of Cartwheel onto seam allowances. Remove templates.

**Cartwheel**

**BACKGROUND**

1. Measure across the center of the cartwheel from outer drawn line to outer drawn line in 3 places (**Fig. 1**). From these measurements, determine the **average diameter**. Divide average diameter by 2 to determine **radius**. For example, the average diameter of **Fig. 1** is 30" and the radius is 15".

**Fig. 1**

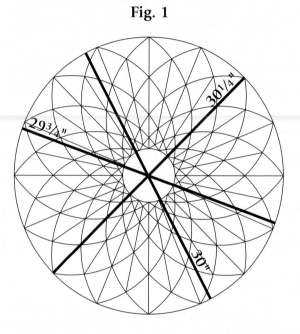

2. To make a background template, refer to **Working With Freezer Paper**, page 6, to join pieces of freezer paper to make a single piece large enough to cut a 35" x 35" square.
3. Fold freezer paper square in half horizontally and vertically and mark center; unfold.

4. Placing point of compass on center mark, use radius to draw a circle. *Note:* To make a compass, tie a length of string to a pencil. Insert a thumbtack in the string at radius. Place tack through center mark of freezer paper square. Holding string taut, draw a circle.

> **TIP** The diameter of the drawn circle should measure the same as the average diameter determined in Step 1.

5. Cut out circle on drawn line; discard circle. The remaining square is your background template. Aligning center opening of template with drawn line of Cartwheel, place template over Cartwheel to check size (**Fig. 2**).

**Fig. 2**

6. If opening of template is too small and points of Cartwheel are cut off, trim opening to the size needed. If opening is too big, repeat Steps 1-5 to re-measure Cartwheel and cut another template.

7. Fold **background square** in half horizontally and vertically and crease; unfold.
8. Aligning crease lines, press background template onto right side of background square (**Fig. 3**).

**Fig. 3**

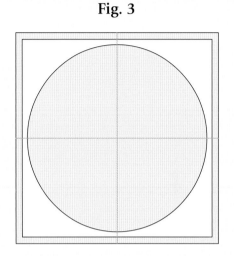

9. Using inner edge of template as a guide and leaving a $^3/_8$" to $^1/_2$" seam allowance, cut out center of background square.
10. With template side down and clipping as needed, press seam allowance to the wrong side around opening (**Fig. 4**).

**Fig. 4**

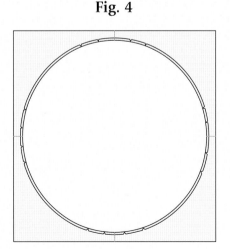

11. Referring to **Quilt Top Center**, match center crease lines of background square with points of Cartwheel and align pressed edge of background square with drawn line of Cartwheel. *Note:* Every 5th point should align with a crease line on background square.

> **TIP**
>
> If opening is too small and points are cut off, press under a wider seam allowance. If opening is too big, press under a smaller seam allowance or you can "float" the Cartwheel by having the pressed edge almost but not quite touch the points of the Cartwheel.

**Quilt Top Center**

12. When satisfied with opening size and placement, glue and then sew background square and cartwheel together to make **Quilt Top Center**. Remove template. Trim Quilt Top Center to 35$\frac{1}{2}$" x 35$\frac{1}{2}$".

13. Refer to **Attaching The Center Oval Or Circle**, page 12, to attach the **center circle** to the Quilt Top Center. Using your preferred method, **Appliqué**, page 73, the center circle in place.

## ADDING THE BORDERS

*Match right sides and use a $\frac{1}{4}$" seam allowance. Refer to **Quilt Diagram** for placement.*

1. Sew 1 **cream small triangle** and 1 yellow polka dot **small triangle** to opposite sides of 1 **square**. Sew 1 yellow polka dot small triangle to each remaining side of corner square to make **Corner Square**. Make 4 Corner Squares. Trim each Corner Square to 4$\frac{1}{2}$" x 4$\frac{1}{2}$".

**Corner Square** (make 4)

2. Remove templates from diamonds, medium triangles and large triangles.

3. Sew 1 cream **large triangle** and 1 yellow polka dot **large triangle** to opposite sides of 1 **diamond** to make **Unit 6**. Make 20 Unit 6's.

**Unit 6** (make 20)

4. Sew 1 cream **medium triangle reversed** and 1 yellow polka dot **medium triangle** to adjacent sides of 1 diamond. Sew 1 yellow polka dot large triangle to the side adjacent to the yellow polka dot medium triangle to make **Unit 7**. Make 4 Unit 7's.

**Unit 7** (make 4)

5. Sew 1 cream **medium triangle reversed** and 1 yellow polka dot medium triangle to adjacent sides of 1 diamond. Sew 1 cream large triangle to the side adjacent to the cream medium triangle to make **Unit 8**. Make 4 Unit 8's.

**Unit 8** (make 4)

6. Sew 5 Unit 6's, 1 Unit 7, and 1 Unit 8 together to make **inner border**. Make 4 inner borders.

**Inner Border** (make 4)

7. Sew **2 inner borders** to opposite sides of the quilt top center.
8. Sew 1 **corner square** to each end of remaining 2 inner borders. Sew inner borders to top and bottom of quilt top center.
9. Sew **top/bottom,** then **side outer borders** to quilt top center to complete **Quilt**.

**Quilt Diagram**

## FINISHING

1. Refer to **Quilting**, page 74, to mark, layer and quilt as desired. The model is outline quilted around the inner border diamonds. The outer border is echo quilted with quilting lines spaced about 1"-2" apart. There is straight-line quilting radiating out from the cartwheel to the inner border. The center circle is quilted with a swirl design.

2. Refer to **Adding A Hanging Sleeve**, page 74, to make and attach a hanging sleeve, if desired.

3. Use **binding square** and refer to **Making A Continuous Bias Strip**, page 77, to make $2^{1}/_{4}$"w bias binding. Refer to **Adding Binding With Mitered Corners**, page 78, to bind quilt.

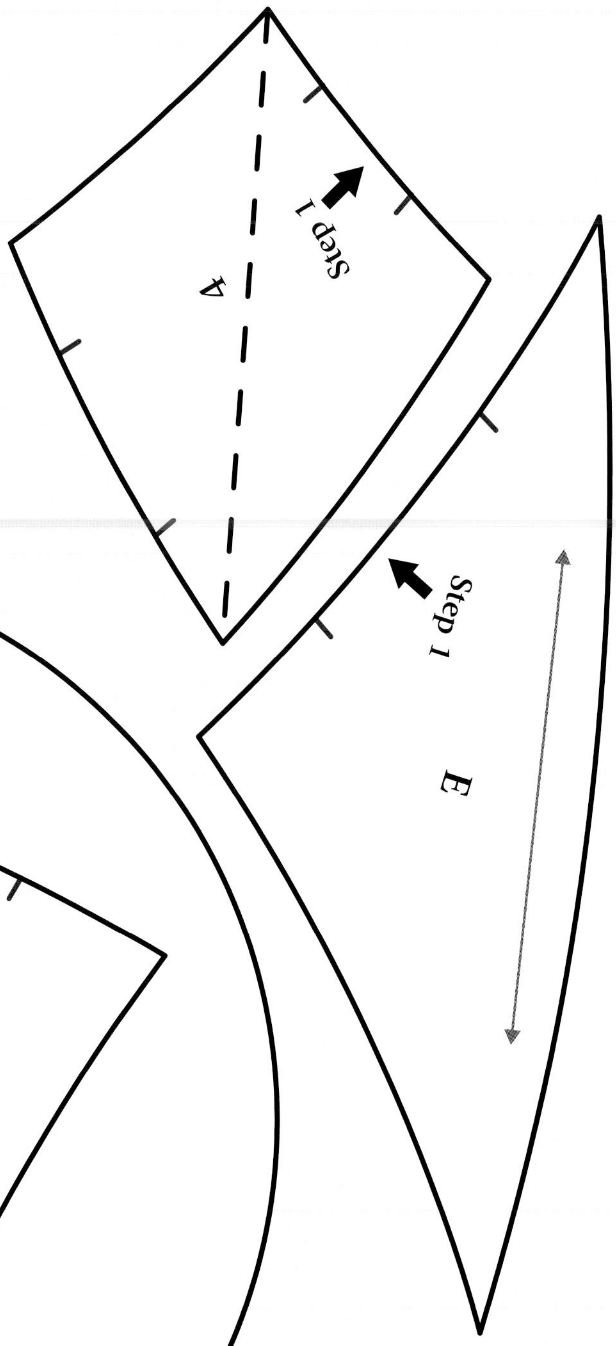

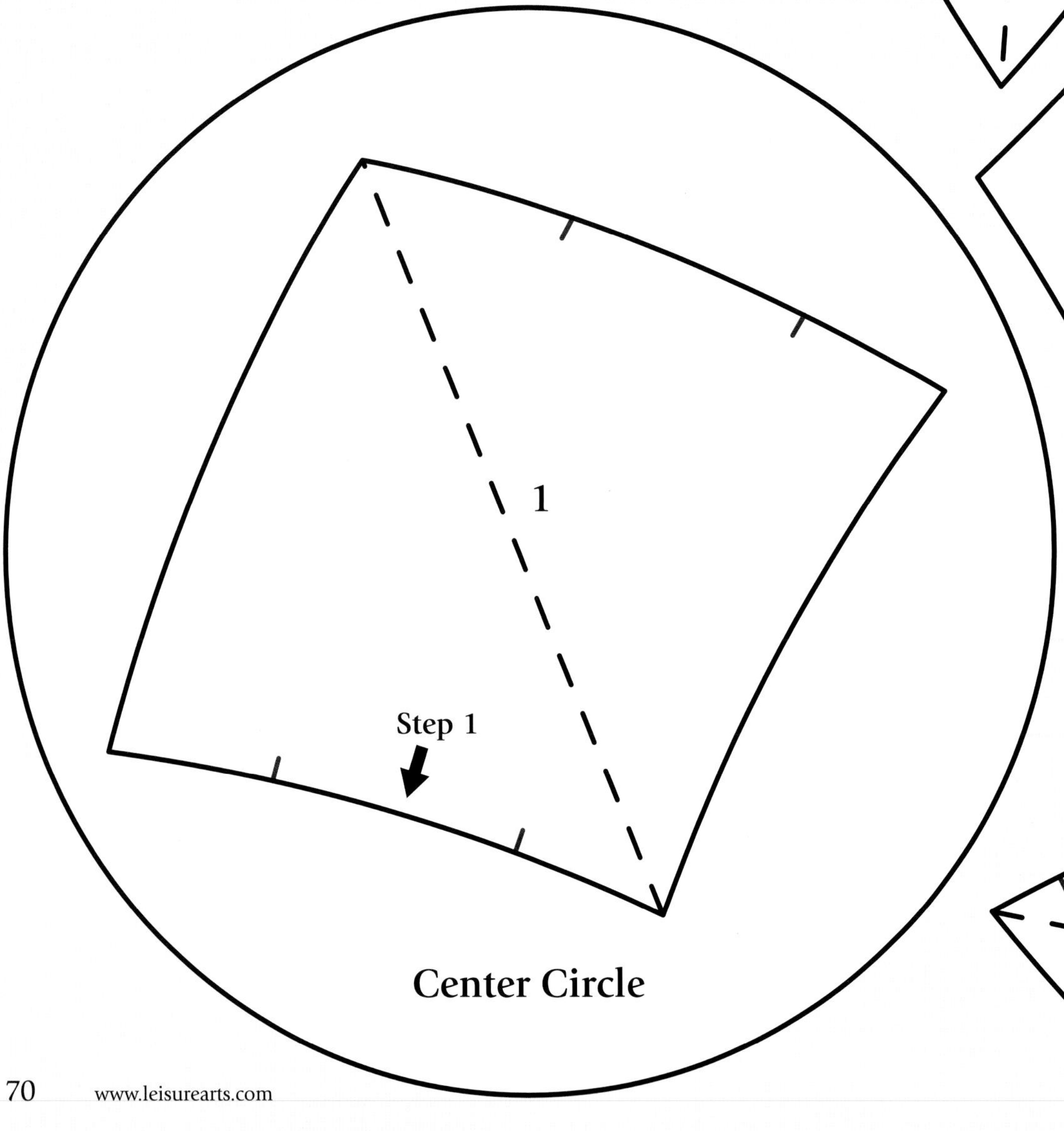

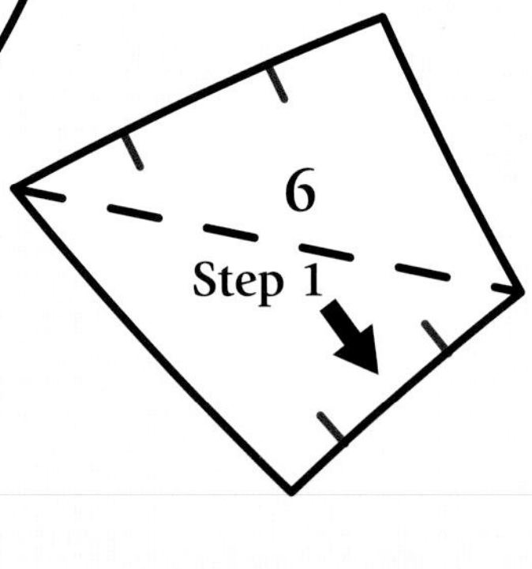

4

Step 1

E

Step 1

1

Step 1

6

Step 1

**Center Circle**

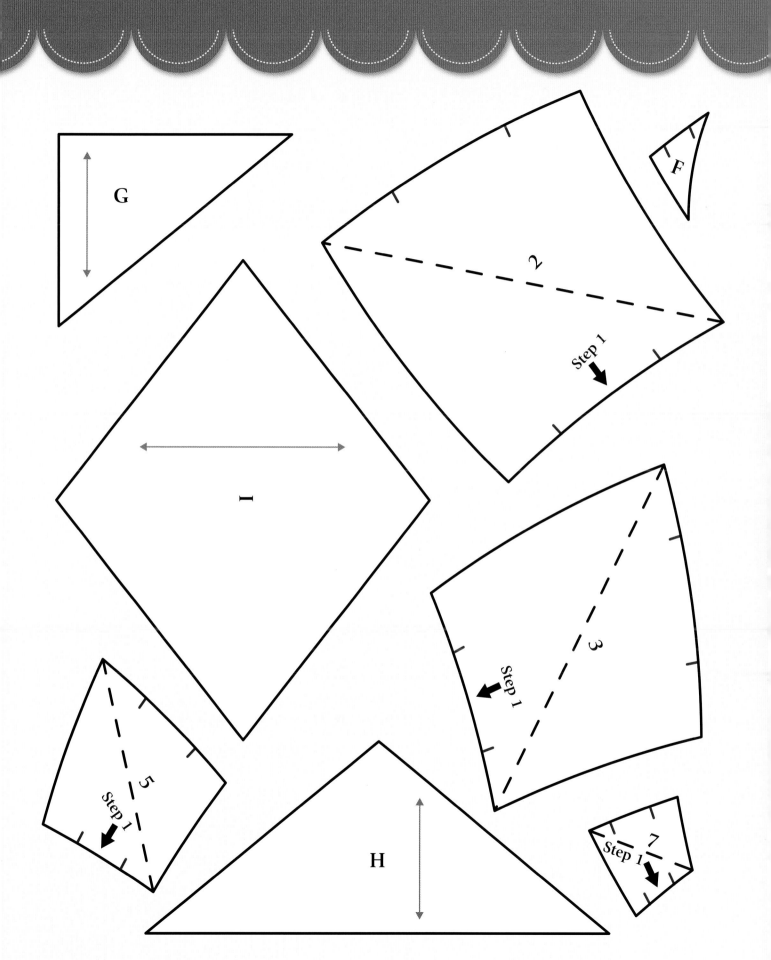

G

F

2

Step 1

I

3

Step 1

5

Step 1

H

7

Step 1

*To make your quilting easier and more enjoyable, carefully read all of the general instructions, study the color photographs, and familiarize yourself with the individual project instructions before beginning a project.*

## FABRICS

Choose high-quality, medium-weight 100% cotton fabrics. All-cotton fabrics hold a crease better, fray less, and are easier to quilt than cotton/ polyester blends.

Yardage requirements listed for each project are based on 43"/44" wide fabric with a "usable" width of 40" after shrinkage and trimming selvages. Actual usable width may vary slightly from fabric to fabric.

We recommend that all fabrics, especially bright and dark colors, be washed, dried, and pressed before cutting. If fabrics are not pre-washed, washing the finished quilt will cause shrinkage and give it a more "antique" look and feel. After washing and drying fabric, fold lengthwise with wrong sides together and matching selvages.

## ROTARY CUTTING

- Place fabric on work surface with fold closest to you.

- Cut all strips from the selvage-to-selvage width of the fabric unless otherwise indicated in project instructions.

- Square left edge of fabric using rotary cutter and rulers (**Figs. 1 - 2**).

**Fig. 1**     **Fig. 2**

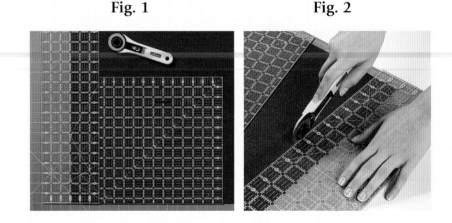

- To cut each strip, place ruler over cut edge of fabric, aligning desired marking on ruler with cut edge; make cut (**Fig. 3**).

**Fig. 3**

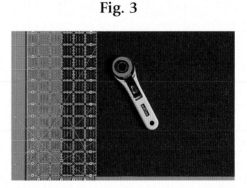

- When cutting several strips from a single piece of fabric, it is important to make sure that cuts remain at a perfect right angle to the fold; square fabric as needed.

## PIECING

*Precise cutting, followed by accurate piecing, will ensure that all pieces of quilt top fit together well.*

- Set sewing machine stitch length for approximately 11 stitches per inch.

- Use neutral-colored general-purpose sewing thread (not quilting thread) in needle and in bobbin.

- Unless otherwise noted in project instructions, always place pieces right sides together and match raw edges; pin if necessary.

- Trim away points of seam allowances that extend beyond edges of sewn pieces.

## SEWING ACROSS SEAM INTERSECTIONS

When sewing across intersection of two seams, place pieces right sides together and match seams exactly, making sure seam allowances are pressed in opposite directions (**Fig. 4**).

**Fig. 4**

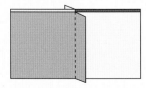

## SEWING SHARP POINTS

To ensure sharp points when joining triangular or diagonal pieces, stitch across the center of the "X" (shown in pink) formed on wrong side by previous seams (**Fig. 5**).

**Fig. 5**

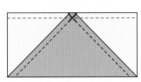

## PRESSING

- Use steam iron set on "Cotton" for all pressing.

- Press after sewing each seam.

- Seam allowances are almost always pressed to one side, usually toward darker fabric. However, to reduce bulk it may occasionally be necessary to press seam allowances toward the lighter fabric or even to press them open.

- To prevent dark fabric seam allowance from showing through light fabric, trim darker seam allowance slightly narrower than lighter seam allowance.

- To press long seams, such as those in long strip sets, without curving or other distortion, lay strips across width of the ironing board.

## APPLIQUÉ

### HAND APPLIQUÉ

1. Thread a sharps needle with a single strand of general-purpose sewing thread that matches appliqué; knot one end.

2. Begin blindstitching (page 80) on as straight an edge as possible. Stitch around entire shape. Take thread to the wrong side, knot and clip thread.

### MACHINE BLANKET STITCH APPLIQUÉ

*Some sewing machines feature a Blanket Stitch similar to the one used in this book. Refer to your owner's manual for machine set-up. If your machine does not have this stitch, try any of the decorative stitches your machine has until you are satisfied with the look.*

1. Thread sewing machine and bobbin with 100% cotton thread in desired weight.

2. Attach an open-toe presser foot. Select far right needle position and needle down (if your machine has these features).

3. If desired, pin a commercial stabilizer to wrong side of background fabric or spray wrong side of background fabric with starch to stabilize.

4. Bring bobbin thread to the top of the fabric by lowering then raising the needle, bringing up the bobbin thread loop. Pull the loop all the way to the surface.

5. Begin by stitching 5 or 6 stitches in place (drop feed dogs or set stitch length at 0), or use your machine's lock stitch feature, if equipped, to anchor thread. Return setting to selected Blanket Stitch.

6. Most of the Blanket Stitch should be done on the appliqué with the right edges of the stitch falling at the very outside edge of the appliqué. Stitch over all exposed raw edges of appliqué pieces.

7. (Note: Dots indicate where to leave needle in fabric when pivoting.) When stitching outside curves (**Fig. 6**), stop with needle down in background fabric. Raise presser foot and pivot project as needed. Lower presser foot and continue stitching, pivoting as often as necessary to follow curve. Small circles may require pivoting between each stitch.

**Fig. 6**

8. When stopping stitching, use a lock stitch to sew 5 or 6 stitches in place or use a needle to pull threads to wrong side of background fabric; knot, then trim ends.

9. Carefully tear away stabilizer, if used.

# QUILTING

*Quilting holds the three layers (top, batting, and backing) of the quilt together. Because marking, layering, and quilting are interrelated and may be done in different orders, please read entire **Quilting** section, pages 74 – 76, before beginning project.*

## TYPES OF QUILTING DESIGNS

### In the Ditch Quilting

Quilting along seamlines or along edges of appliquéd pieces is called "in the ditch" quilting. This type of quilting should be done on side **opposite** seam allowance and does not have to be marked.

### Outline Quilting

Quilting a consistent distance, usually $1/4$", from seam or appliqué is called "outline" quilting. Outline quilting may be marked, or $1/4$" wide masking tape may be placed along seamlines for quilting guide. (Do not leave tape on quilt longer than necessary, since it may leave an adhesive residue.)

### Echo Quilting

Quilting that follows the outline of an appliquéd or pieced design with two or more parallel lines is called "echo" quilting. This type of quilting does not need to be marked.

### Meandering Quilting

Quilting in random curved lines and swirls is called "meandering" quilting. Quilting lines should not cross or touch each other. This type of quilting does not need to be marked.

### Stipple Quilting

Meandering quilting that is very closely spaced is called "stipple" quilting. Stippling will flatten the area quilted and is often stitched in background areas to raise appliquéd or pieced designs. This type of quilting does not need to be marked.

## MARKING QUILTING LINES

Quilting lines may be marked using fabric marking pencils, chalk markers, or water- or air-soluble pens. A wide variety of pre-cut quilting stencils, as well as entire books of quilting patterns, are available.

Simple quilting designs may be marked with chalk or chalk pencil after basting. A small area may be marked, then quilted, before moving to next area to be marked. Intricate designs should be marked before basting using a more durable marker.

*Caution:* Pressing may permanently set some marks. **Test** different markers **on scrap fabric** to find one that marks clearly and can be thoroughly removed.

## PREPARING THE BACKING

*To allow for slight shifting of quilt top during quilting, backing should be approximately 4" larger on all sides for large quilts and 2" on all sides for small quilts. Yardage requirements listed for quilt backings are calculated for 43"/44"w fabric. To piece a backing, use the following instructions.*

1.  Measure length and width of quilt top; add 8" (4") to each measurement.
2.  Cut backing fabric into two lengths slightly longer than determined *length* measurement. Trim selvages. Place lengths with right sides facing and sew long edges together, forming tube (**Fig. 7**). Match seams and press along one fold (**Fig. 8**). Cut along pressed fold to form single piece (**Fig. 9**).

| Fig. 7 | Fig. 8 | Fig. 9 |
| --- | --- | --- |

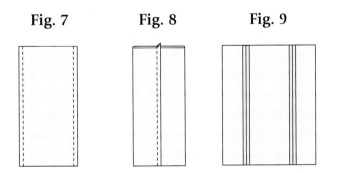

3.  Trim backing to size determined in Step 1; press seam allowances open.

## CHOOSING THE BATTING

The appropriate batting will make quilting easier. All cotton or cotton/ polyester blend battings work well for machine quilting because the cotton helps "grip" quilt layers. Fusible batting works well for small projects such as placemats, pillows, or table runners.

When selecting batting, refer to package labels for characteristics and care instructions. Cut batting same size as prepared backing.

## ASSEMBLING THE QUILT

1.  Examine wrong side of quilt top closely; trim any seam allowances and clip any threads that may show through front of the quilt. Press quilt top, being careful not to "set" any marked quilting lines.
2.  Place backing *wrong* side up on flat surface. Use masking tape to tape edges of backing to surface. Place batting on top of backing fabric. Smooth batting gently, being careful not to stretch or tear. Center quilt top *right* side up on batting.
3.  Use 1" rustproof safety pins to "pin-baste" all layers together, spacing pins approximately 4" apart. Begin at center and work toward outer edges to secure all layers. If possible, place pins away from areas that will be quilted, although pins may be removed as needed when quilting.

## MACHINE QUILTING METHODS

Use general-purpose thread in bobbin. Do not use quilting thread. Thread the needle of machine with a neutral color general-purpose thread to make quilting blend with quilt top fabrics. Use decorative thread, such as a metallic or contrasting-color general-purpose thread, to make quilting lines stand out more.

### Straight-Line Quilting

*The term "straight-line" is somewhat deceptive, since curves (especially gentle ones) as well as straight lines can be stitched with this technique.*

1. Set stitch length for six to ten stitches per inch and attach walking foot to sewing machine.
2. Determine which section of quilt will have longest continuous quilting line, oftentimes the area from center top to center bottom. Roll up and secure each edge of quilt to help reduce the bulk, keeping fabrics smooth. Smaller projects may not need to be rolled.
3. Begin stitching on longest quilting line, using very short stitches for the first $1/4$" to "lock" quilting. Stitch across project, using one hand on each side of walking foot to slightly spread fabric and to guide fabric through machine. Lock stitches at end of quilting line.
4. Continue machine quilting, stitching longer quilting lines first to stabilize quilt before moving on to other areas.

### Free-Motion Quilting

*Free-motion quilting may be free form or may follow a marked pattern.*

1. Attach darning foot to sewing machine and lower or cover feed dogs.
2. Position quilt under darning foot; lower foot. Holding top thread, take a stitch and pull bobbin thread to top of quilt. To "lock" beginning of quilting line, hold top and bobbin threads while making three to five stitches in place.
3. Use one hand on each side of darning foot to slightly spread fabric and to move fabric through the machine. Even stitch length is achieved by using smooth, flowing hand motion and steady machine speed. Slow machine speed and fast hand movement will create long stitches. Fast machine speed and slow hand movement will create short stitches. Move quilt sideways, back and forth, in a circular motion, or in a random motion to create desired designs; do not rotate quilt. Lock stitches at end of each quilting line.

## MAKING A HANGING SLEEVE

*Attaching a hanging sleeve to back of wall hanging or quilt before the binding is added allows project to be displayed on wall.*

1. Measure width of quilt top edge and subtract 1". Cut piece of fabric 7"w by determined measurement.
2. Press short edges of fabric piece $1/4$" to wrong side; press edges $1/4$" to wrong side again and machine stitch in place.
3. Matching wrong sides, fold piece in half lengthwise to form tube.
4. Follow project instructions to sew binding to quilt top and to trim backing and batting. Before Blindstitching binding to backing, match raw edges and stitch hanging sleeve to center top edge on back of quilt.
5. Finish binding quilt, treating hanging sleeve as part of backing.
6. Blindstitch, page 80, bottom of hanging sleeve to backing, taking care not to stitch through to front of quilt.

## MAKING A CONTINUOUS BIAS STRIP

*Bias strips for binding or piping can simply be cut and pieced to desired length. However, when a long length is needed, the "continuous" method is quick and accurate.*

1. Use piping or binding square indicated in project instructions. Cut square in half diagonally to make two triangles.
2. With right sides together and using $1/4$" seam allowance, sew triangles together (**Fig. 10**); press seam allowances open.

**Fig. 10**

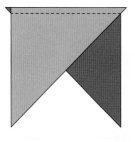

3. On wrong side of fabric, draw lines $2^1/4$" apart (**Fig. 11**). Cut off any remaining fabric less than this width.

**Fig. 11**

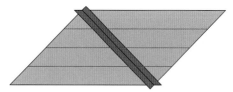

4. With right sides inside, bring short edges together to form tube; match raw edges so that first drawn line of top section meets second drawn line of bottom section (**Fig. 12**).

**Fig. 12**

5. Carefully pin edges together by inserting pins through drawn lines at point where drawn lines intersect, making sure pins go through intersections on both sides. Using $1/4$" seam allowance, sew edges together; press seam allowances open.
6. To cut continuous strip, begin cutting along first drawn line (**Fig. 13**). Continue cutting along drawn line around tube.

**Fig. 13**

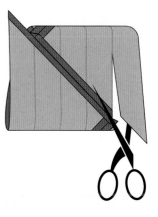

7. Trim ends of bias strip to square.
8. Matching wrong sides and raw edges, carefully press bias strip in half lengthwise to complete binding.

# BINDING

## ATTACHING BINDING WITH MITERED CORNERS

1. Beginning with one end near center on bottom edge of quilt, lay binding around quilt to make sure that seams in binding will not end up at a corner. Adjust placement if necessary. Matching raw edges of binding to raw edge of quilt top, pin binding to right side of quilt along one edge.

2. When you reach first corner, mark $^1/_4$" from corner of quilt top (**Fig. 14**).

**Fig. 14**

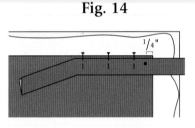

3. Beginning approximately 10" from end of binding and using $^1/_4$" seam allowance, sew binding to quilt, backstitching at beginning of stitching and at mark (**Fig. 15**). Lift needle out of fabric and clip thread.

**Fig. 15**

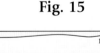
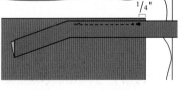

4. Fold binding as shown in **Figs. 16 – 17** and pin binding to adjacent side, matching raw edges. When you've reached the next corner, mark $^1/_4$" from edge of quilt top.

**Fig. 16**          **Fig. 17**

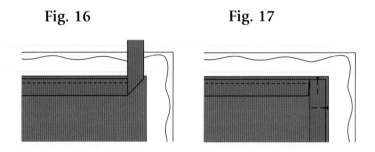

5. Backstitching at edge of quilt top, sew pinned binding to quilt (**Fig. 18**); backstitch at the next mark. Lift needle out of fabric and clip thread.

**Fig. 18**

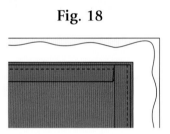

6. Continue sewing binding to quilt, stopping approximately 10" from starting point (**Fig. 19**).

**Fig. 19**

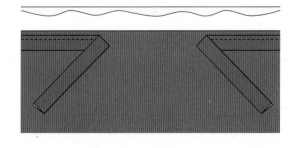

7. Bring beginning and end of binding to center of opening and fold each end back, leaving a ¹/₄" space between folds (**Fig. 20**). Finger press folds.

**Fig. 20**

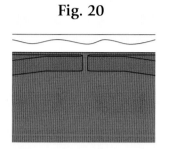

8. Unfold ends of binding and draw a line across wrong side in finger-pressed crease. Draw a line through the lengthwise pressed fold of binding at the same spot to create a cross mark. With edge of ruler at cross mark, line up 45˚ angle marking on ruler with one long side of binding. Draw a diagonal line from edge to edge. Repeat on remaining end, making sure that the two diagonal lines are angled the same way (**Fig. 21**).

**Fig. 21**

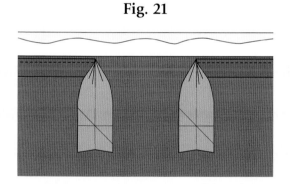

9. Matching right sides and diagonal lines, pin binding ends together at right angles (**Fig. 22**).

**Fig. 22**

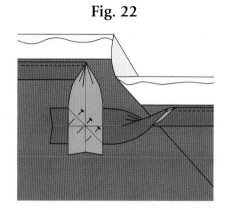

10. Machine stitch along diagonal line (**Fig. 23**), removing pins as you stitch.

**Fig. 23**

11. Lay binding against quilt to double check that it is correct length.
12. Trim binding ends, leaving ¹/₄" seam allowance; press seam open. Stitch binding to quilt.
13. Trim backing and batting a scant ¹/₄" larger than quilt top so that batting and backing will fill the binding when it is folded over to quilt backing.

14. On one edge of quilt, fold binding over to quilt backing and pin pressed edge in place, covering stitching line (**Fig. 24**). On adjacent side, fold binding over, forming a mitered corner (**Fig. 25**). Repeat to pin remainder of binding in place.

**Fig. 24**        **Fig. 25**

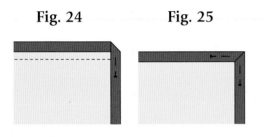

15. Blindstitch binding to backing, taking care not to stitch through to front of quilt.

## ATTACHING BINDING (CELTIC KNOT)

1. Beginning with one end near center on bottom edge of quilt and matching raw edges of binding to raw edge of quilt top, pin binding to right side of quilt.
2. Beginning approximately 10" from end of binding and backstitching at beginning of stitching and use a ¹/₄" seam allowance to sew binding to quilt, stopping approximately 10" from starting point (**Fig. 19**).
3. Follow **Steps 7-13** of **Attaching Binding With Mitered Corners**, page 79.
4. Fold binding over to quilt backing and pin pressed edge in place, covering stitching line. Blindstitch binding to backing, taking care not to stitch through to front of quilt.

## BLIND STITCH

Come up at 1, go down at 2, and come up at 3. Length of stitches may be varied as desired.

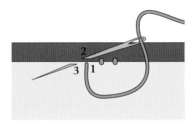

| Metric Conversion Chart | |
|---|---|
| Inches x 2.54 = centimeters (cm) | Yards x .9144 = meters (m) |
| Inches x 25.4 = millimeters (mm) | Yards x 91.44 = centimeters (cm) |
| Inches x .0254 = meters (m) | Centimeters x .3937 = inches (") |
| | Meters x 1.0936 = yards (yd) |

| Standard Equivalents | | | | | |
|---|---|---|---|---|---|
| ¹/₈" | 3.2 mm | 0.32 cm | ¹/₈ yard | 11.43 cm | 0.11 m |
| ¹/₄" | 6.35 mm | 0.635 cm | ¹/₄ yard | 22.86 cm | 0.23 m |
| ³/₈" | 9.5 mm | 0.95 cm | ³/₈ yard | 34.29 cm | 0.34 m |
| ¹/₂" | 12.7 mm | 1.27 cm | ¹/₂ yard | 45.72 cm | 0.46 m |
| ⁵/₈" | 15.9 mm | 1.59 cm | ⁵/₈ yard | 57.15 cm | 0.57 m |
| ³/₄" | 19.1 mm | 1.91 cm | ³/₄ yard | 68.58 cm | 0.69 m |
| ⁷/₈" | 22.2 mm | 2.22 cm | ⁷/₈ yard | 80 cm | 0.8 m |
| 1" | 25.4 mm | 2.54 cm | 1 yard | 91.44 cm | 0.91 m |